Read,
Write, Spell

Read, Write, Spell

Wendy Bean
and
Chrys Bouffler

Stenhouse Publishers
YORK, MAINE

Stenhouse Publishers, 431 York Street, York, Maine 03909

ISBN 1-57110-075-X

First published simultaneously in 1997 in the United States
by Stenhouse and in Australia by
Eleanor Curtain Publishing
906 Malvern Road
Armadale Vic 3134
Australia

Production by Publishing Solutions
Edited by Ruth Siems
Text design by David Constable
Cover photograph by Jim Whitney
Printed in Australia

Contents

Introduction

Has anything changed?

Ask people in the street about literacy and most will tell you that standards are declining. Almost invariably the first 'evidence' advanced is that today, children and school leavers cannot spell. Other things such as grammar also come in for criticism, but spelling looms large in the 'public' perception of what it means to be literate. The public perceives that standards of spelling are declining and that it is somehow the fault of schools for not teaching spelling.

Even if these perceptions are accepted at face value, several questions must be asked: Against what standard is this decline being measured? When was the golden age when nearly all children left school able to spell? Our search for an answer has led us to a variety of insights into spelling and the teaching of spelling but, alas, not to the discovery of that golden age. We are forced to conclude that no such time existed. In fact, there has hardly been a time in recent history when spelling standards, in one form or another, were not the subject of comment or debate.

Arguments for standardisation and reform of English spelling range from Richard Mulcaster's call for 'right writing' in his *Elementaire* of 1582, through Noah Webster's attempts to develop an American spelling in his dictionary first published in 1783, to the abortive attempt to pass a Simplified Spelling Bill through the British House of Commons in 1945, and on to the present day. For example, Valerie Yule (1995) argues for spelling reform, suggesting that the intransigence of English spelling may well give way before the onslaught of modern technology.

Resistance to reform was largely born of social attitudes to spelling. Such attitudes persist even to this day. Echoes of Lord Chesterfield's admonition of his son can be found in many a letter to the editor on matters of spelling. Chesterfield wrote:

> I come to another part of your letter, which is the orthography, if I may call bad spelling orthography. You spell induce, <u>educe</u>; and grandeur you spell <u>grandure</u>, two faults of which few of my housemaids would have been guilty. I must tell you that orthography, in the true sense of the word, is so absolutely necessary for a man of letters, or a gentleman, that one false spelling may fix a ridicule on him for the rest of his life; and I know a man of quality who never recovered from the ridicule of having wholesome without the <u>w</u>. (*Letters to His Son 1737–57*, vol. 4, p. 1620)

Along with the advent of compulsory public education in the 19th century and the entrenched social attitudes to spelling came the concern for its teaching. It was during this period that spelling came to occupy a large part of the school curriculum, a position it has maintained to the present day. We asked a number of teachers what their memories of spelling were. Almost all could remember memorising lists of words, Friday spelling and dictation, and regular classroom exercises involving rules such as *i* before *e* except after *c*. Several mentioned the pressure to 'get it right' and the sense of success and/or failure. Spelling bees, those peculiarly Anglo-American forms of competitive knowledge display, also loomed large in their memory.

> I remember spelling lists – theme words and phonic tests.

> Spelling lists (meaningless!) Friday spelling tests. Daily 'Round Robin' oral testing!

> We had to get every word right. I felt pressured.

> Competitive. Gold stars. Spelling bees. Spelling champ.

> I don't remember. I guess there was a lot of rote learning but I am a good speller … I guess that if you had trouble spelling it would really stick in your mind – but if it's easy then you just enjoy it.

Despite the amount of time devoted to spelling in the school curriculum, student success in learning appears to have been limited. In an article in the *Brisbane Daily Standard*, 4 October 1917, the writer complained:

> Reading lacks fluency, articulation is defective … Spelling has not reached a high standard … Grammar is the bugbear of most teachers and children … Even writing has not reached a satisfactory stage. 'Back to the 3 R's' will be the necessary slogan if improvement does not soon show up.

Seventy-seven years later in the *Sunday Age*, 17 July 1994, under the banner: 'Why one in seven students can't read', the following claims were made about spelling:

> Up to 15% of children are leaving school unable to read or spell properly because of the way reading is taught in primary schools …

> Schools are under pressure to reintroduce phonics because kids are coming out of schools who can't read and spell …

> Teachers stopped correcting spelling and punctuation because this might quell students' enthusiasm for reading and writing …

The same demand for a return to 'basics' is prevalent today, so have more recent changes taken place in the teaching of spelling? Our questioning of teachers revealed that they, like the general public, demand high levels of spelling accuracy from school leavers. Nevertheless, they displayed a greater tolerance of 'invented' spelling in the early grades. Personal spelling lists and dictionaries had replaced set lists in these grades. While most reported helping children to use a variety of strategies including sight words, letter patterns, spelling rules, silent letters and sounding out, there was certainly no evidence that spelling was not being taught. In fact, spelling remained a major concern. Our observations suggest that traditional approaches still dominate the upper primary and secondary sector and are also to be found in many lower primary classrooms.

Some myths and misconceptions

While current beliefs and attitudes to spelling remain, those who are unable to attain high levels of spelling accuracy will always be seen as less than totally literate and 'a problem' requiring some kind of remedy. This is despite the fact that many highly successful individuals, including published writers, have what we would call 'spelling problems'. Many current attitudes are based on ignorance of the nature and purpose of spelling. Some of these 'myths' and misconceptions about spelling are worth examining.

MYTH 1: ENGLISH SPELLING IS CHAOTIC

George Bernard Shaw once claimed that English spelling was so chaotic that you could spell 'fish' *ghoti* – *gh* as in 'enough', *o* as in 'women', and *ti* as in 'nation'. However, it is highly unlikely that any writer of the language, even one of questionable spelling ability, would spell 'fish' in this way. Intuitively all English language users know that 'gh' in the initial position never says 'f' and 'ti' never says 'sh' unless it is in a word ending with 'tion'. To put it another way, writers of English know the rules of English orthography. These are the rules which govern the way we spell and which render spelling systematic. If there were no system there would be no written form of English.

While it is true that English spelling has its idiosyncrasies, it is about 80% phonetically regular. Language changes over time; if it did not we would be dealing with a dead language like Latin. Written language changes at a slower rate than spoken language which results in mismatches between the spelling of some words and their modern-day pronunciations. Still other words are borrowings from other languages. Most idiosyncrasies can be explained by historical factors or by borrowings.

There are two important misconceptions associated with the myth of chaos:

(i) Spelling should be reformed to reflect pronunciation

This view considers spelling only as a part of writing, not as an aspect of written language involved in both reading and writing. While phonetic spelling may remove some idiosyncrasies that create problems for writers, it does not necessarily help readers. Pronunciation varies, and is very susceptible to change. The various dialects of the United Kingdom are testimony to this, but even in Australia it is possible to discern differences in pronunciation and other aspects of language from state to state. Given the variety of English pronunciation, whose pronunciation would be the basis of reform?

Spelling phonetically creates its own set of problems. Consider, for example, what happens to the vowel sound in the following set of related words:

harm<u>o</u>ny   harm<u>o</u>nic   harm<u>o</u>nious

Changing the representation of the vowel to reflect the sound would destroy the visually signalled relationship of meaning between these words. In the same way, if 'sign' were spelled, say, 'sine', the visual meaning relationship of that word to words such as 'signal' and 'signature' would be lost. It is in the interest of readers that these meaning connections be maintained.

There is no doubt that some spelling could be altered without affecting the needs of readers. Spelling has undergone changes even within our lifetime; nevertheless, a strong case can be made for accelerating some of this change. The English writing system is one of the few major written language systems that has not undergone an update in the last hundred years. However, the notion that spelling should reflect pronunciation ignores both the necessarily complex nature of any writing system and the unstable nature of pronunciation.

(ii) The only way spelling can be learnt is by memorisation

This is the most pervasive and insidious of all misconceptions about spelling, and one that the education system has perpetuated over the years through its approaches to teaching spelling. Judging by community reactions to attempts to teach spelling by means other than spelling lists, it is a cycle not easily broken. If children are not given lists of words then they are not being taught spelling.

Although we have come some way in our understanding of language in recent years, the spelling lists that children are expected to memorise are still very much alive and well. How spelling may best be learnt is discussed in the following chapter so will not be pursued here. However, it is worth noting that given the extent of the average person's vocabulary, it would be a mental feat beyond imagining to memorise and not forget the spelling of the vast majority of those words. Anyone who has had to memorise lines for a play will know how difficult it is, and how easy to forget them once the play is finished. Yet you may well write today a word you have not used for years and spell it correctly. Clearly learning to spell involves very complex language learning.

MYTH 2: THERE IS ONLY ONE WAY TO SPELL – THE RIGHT WAY!

Richard Mulcaster, writing in 1582, talks of 'the right writing of our English tung', while the Oxford dictionary some four hundred years later defines spelling in terms of a 'standard of right writing'. The fact that the spelling used by Mulcaster and the spelling found in a modern Oxford reveal not inconsiderable differences tells us much about the nature of spelling. There is simply more than one way to spell any word in English.

All language is a complex set of social conventions. However, it is useful to think of the conventions that relate to the rules of language as linguistic conventions. In the case of spelling, these conventions are the orthographic and phonological rules which determine what sounds are represented and what letters or letter combinations represent them. English orthography may not allow *ghoti* as a spelling for 'fish' but it does allow such spellings as *fysh, physh, fiche* and so on. The fact that the word referring to a marine creature is generally spelled as *fish* is a matter of usage. Such usage may vary with context. In the context of a person or place name, *fysh* is the more likely spelling.

Standard spelling – the spelling we think of as right spelling – is as much a matter of usage as of linguistic convention. Put simply, standard spelling is that spelling, out of all possible spellings of a word, which a community decides to use. Standard American spelling is not necessarily the same as standard English spelling. What is acceptable, or standard, in the world of advertising is not necessarily acceptable in other contexts such as education. Spelling can also be used to make political statements, for example by spelling 'women' as 'wimin'.

(i) Spelling is automatic

This misconception grows out of the myth of one spelling. Once you know the standard form you will use it as a matter of habit. This denies the fact that spelling is an aspect of language, and that all language is context specific. The situation in which we write affects not only how we write but how we spell. Note-taking is one of the more obvious examples: the way we might spell in that situation differs from how we would spell when writing a formal letter. It is highly likely that spelling during note-taking, as when making a shopping list, will contain a proportion of non-standard spellings and personal abbreviations.

Spelling, like reading and writing, involves the use of semantic, syntactic and graphophonic cues. To suggest that spelling is simply a matter of learning sounds is ridiculous. Try to sound out *yacht, laugh, knife, sure, tough* and *women,* to list a few examples. Clearly other spelling strategies are needed.

Knowing the difference between *principal* and *principle, their* and *there* requires more than phonics. It is interesting to speculate on what spelling strategies the news reader who, in an item about a body found on a beach, referred to an *auto spy* being conducted, would adopt to spell 'autopsy'. Clearly the news reader had no knowledge of the word and its meaning. Meaning is at the root of all language, and at the root of spelling. Given this complexity, spelling can never be automatic.

(ii) Good spellers never make mistakes

This misconception is also associated with the belief in right spelling. It is a rather dysfunctional view, often held even by very young writers. In fact, the more you write the more likely you are to misspell words, no matter how good a speller you may consider yourself. This is a natural part of language use. We accept miscues as part of reading but are less willing to accept misspelling as part of writing. Most standard spellers are able to identify misspellings, if they see them, when they reread their writing, but proofreading is not a simple matter even for good spellers. To understand why this might be so, we need to reflect briefly on the reading process.

It is generally recognised that we do not read word for word. There are many explanations for what happens when we read but the most widely accepted, from a cognitive perspective, is that reading involves prediction. We scan the page and, from the information coming to our brain, we predict meaning. Our predictions are either confirmed or corrected as we continue scanning. Sometimes our predictions do not match exactly what is on the page. If these mismatches or miscues maintain meaning and there is nothing in the information coming to the brain from our scanning that causes us to question our prediction, then we are likely to continue our reading unaware that there has been any miscue.

A large number of cognitive, social and cultural factors are involved in making a text readable. Put simply, however, the more knowledge of the subject, the syntax and style of the writer we bring to a text the easier it is to read. Alternatively, the more predictable a text is the easier it is to read because it requires us to take up less visual information from the page in order to construct the meaning. This is why repeated readings of the same story with young children are important for their reading development, and this is the theory behind predictable books that have repeated or cumulative patterns of meaning. However, the most predictable text you can read is one you have written yourself. This means that when you read your text, especially when you have just written it, you require less visual information from the page to reconstruct meaning and, therefore, it is likely that you will not see some non-standard spellings even though you are entirely familiar with the standard forms.

There are often complaints about the poor spelling ability of students at university. From observations of student writing behaviour, we would hazard a guess that in many cases the problem lies not with the students' spelling ability but with writing practices. The essay is due in a 5 pm and at 5 minutes to 5 the student adds the finishing touches, gives a quick read through, and into the box it goes. It is almost guaranteed that the student will receive the essay back with some comment about spelling.

How often is spelling the first aspect of a child's text that is addressed? Putting some time between the writing and the proofreading of a text assists proofreading but does not guarantee that even good standard spellers will see their misspellings. The standards of spelling that society demands are extremely high – one is tempted to say almost impossibly so.

MYTH 3: SPELLING IS THE BENCHMARK OF LITERACY

This myth is inherent in much of our discussion of social attitudes to spelling. Reading and writing are associated with the power relations and values of a society, and Lord Chesterfield's letter is a good illustration of values associated with spelling use. Over the last century, the attainments required to be an 'educated' person in the classical sense have been altered and eroded by the rise of the sciences and the steady rise of the school leaving age. When everybody can read and write, how is an 'educated' person to be distinguished from the masses? Insistence on high levels of spelling accuracy is one way that present-day society restricts entry into the class of the 'educated' elite.

The public view of literacy is still that of an acquired set of technical skills. Many educators, however, recognise it as much more complex. Today we talk not of literacy but of literacies, recognising the role of social and cultural contexts in determining what counts as literacy. We may appear more or less literate depending on the context. The inability of individuals to reach the high levels of spelling accuracy demanded does not necessarily render them illiterate. There are those who have ignored social attitudes and, despite problems with spelling, have gone on to become highly successful experts in their field. Some have made successful livings from their writing. They would be judged highly literate by their peers.

1

Learning to spell

For the 6092 one- and two-syllable words used by 6–9 year olds, there are 211 distinct spelling sound 'correspondences'. For these words there are 60 rules for the consonants and 23 exceptions, 106 rules for vowels and 22 exceptions. (Frank Smith 1978, p. 170)

Spelling is not separate from reading and writing

Most of us would agree academically that writing is far more than spelling, yet in many cases our practices give lie to our understanding. Spelling consumes a large amount of teaching time, often more than is devoted to the teaching of writing itself. Even where the teaching of writing appears paramount, very often the first thing teachers turn to when assessing children's written products is spelling. Parents generally expect that spelling will be taught separately. There are many who believe that unless children learn to use standard spelling they cannot learn to write, and unless they have spelling lists and a separate time in the weekly curriculum for teaching and testing they are not being taught spelling.

In the real world, spelling is not isolated from reading or writing. Only in school does this happen. The process of writing includes the process of reading. During writing, the writer switches mental stance between that of writer and that of reader. When you are in the act of composing a piece of text it is likely that you have the mental stance of a writer, but there comes a point when you stand back from your writing and view it as a reader before re-engaging in writing. This may be easier to appreciate if the writing process is represented diagrammatically (see figure 1).

Figure 1: The writing process

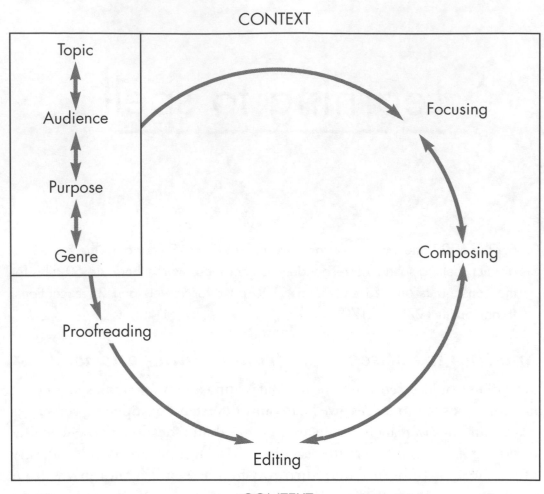

When you start to write, you select a global **focus** for your writing then, as you write, this focus narrows to the first word, the first sentence and so on. Gradually the global focus becomes refined and the text and its meaning takes shape. The process of developing the text we refer to as **composing**. During composing we adjust the text, shaping and reshaping what we want to say. This process we call **editing**. Editing involves mentally switching between the stances of reader and writer. This switching often occurs many times and is particularly evident when children are writing. Finally, if the audience and purpose of our text demand it, we may stand outside the text and quite deliberately assume the stance of a reader and **proofread** our text. It is not insignificant that we call this aspect of the process *proofreading* and not *proof writing*.

During writing, when the focus is on the composing, a writer is likely to use whatever spelling is most functional at the time. During reading, however, the writer is more likely to have a heightened awareness of editorial concerns, including spelling. When proofreading, the concern for standard spelling and other surface features of language becomes paramount. A writer may well confuse 'there' and 'their' when writing, but have no difficulty in distinguishing between the two when reading. In short, spelling may vary between the contexts of reading and writing.

READING, WRITING AND SPELLING

The belief that you cannot write unless you can use standard spelling may, on the face of it, have some validity. Certainly you need some kind of spelling system in order to write; without a system it is not possible to reconstruct meaning over time. While standard spelling is systematic, spelling does not have to be standard to be read. Many historical documents have variable spellings yet their meaning is accessible. Teachers often have no difficulty reading children's early writing although much of its spelling is non-standard. The following is a good example:

> Dear Mr Halley
>
> The comet zat you have predicted haes kaem true You comet crmez around evre 76 years I have neet sen Halleys my mum reckons zat ther best tiem is next month.

Spelling develops as a consequence of engaging in the process of writing, and we would also assert that spelling develops as a consequence of reading. In fact you must be a reader in order to be a writer. This is not to say that one precedes the other but, rather, that reading, writing and spelling develop simultaneously and in transaction with each other.

Approaches to spelling

The major approaches to teaching spelling, which have persisted over many years, include the list approach, the rule-based approach and morphographic spelling. Hundreds of schemes and programs have been produced using these approaches. However, because of our belief that learning to spell is part of the complex process of language learning, implicated in both reading and writing, we will be advocating an integrated approach.

A traditional list approach to spelling requires children to memorise lists of words provided by the teacher or through a spelling scheme. Originally the teaching strategy involved only memorisation and testing, but over the years some major list approaches have also included worksheets with a variety of activities using the words in the list. Usually there is no particular reason for the choice of the words. At best, the list is based on dated research into the most commonly used words, spelling demons and the like. Teachers using a list approach may also select words from curriculum areas and from the children's writing. The issue then becomes how the list is learnt and the appropriateness of the selected words.

A rule-based approach involves teaching particular spelling rules and then having children apply these in their writing. Generally the rules are memorised. While learning particular rules can sometimes be useful, the exceptions become complicated and the number of rules makes a daunting learning task.

Morphographic spelling forms the basis of many direct instruction programs over the years and involves phonemic, morphemic and whole-word approaches. Sound–symbol correspondences based on morphemic units are taught in sequence, daily and often to the whole class. Success is often 'guaranteed' by the authors, provided the program of scripted lessons is closely followed.

Despite these approaches, many students leave school seemingly unable to reach the standard of spelling demanded by society. The reasons for this are many and complex, but we do not believe that the answer to the problem can be found in returning to traditional methods which isolate spelling from language and make it a matter of memorising words and rules. There is no reason to believe that methods which have failed in the past will work in the future. In the 1990s we know more about how spelling is learnt, the complexity of the task and the relationship between reading, writing and spelling. For these reasons, we believe that an integrated approach is necessary.

For those who have abandoned schemes, the practice of an integrated approach is to draw words from the children's own reading and writing activities and to use these as demonstrations of particular aspects of spelling as the need arises. This involves setting up audiences for writing, and focusing on the need to proofread as appropriate to the audience and purpose for the writing.

Spelling as part of language learning

We can only begin to understand how children learn to spell if we consider spelling as an aspect of language, and learning to spell as part of the overall process of learning language.

There is much that can be said about language, but ultimately there are three key principles which are crucial to our understanding of language (Halliday 1984):

- **Language is FUNCTIONAL.** Language is used for a purpose and that purpose is to mean. We use language to classify and organise our world, to communicate.

- **Language is SOCIAL.** People use language. It is brought into being in the dialogue between speakers and listeners, readers and writers. It is people who establish patterns of usage and decide what is acceptable and what is not.

- **Language is CONTEXTUAL.** Language occurs in particular contexts which affect the way it is used and understood.

They same key principles apply to spelling:

- **Spelling is FUNCTIONAL.** It serves the purposes of readers and writers in making meaning, although these purposes are not entirely similar. What serves the writer's purpose does not necessarily serve the reader's purpose.

- **Spelling is SOCIAL.** Spelling, like all language, is related to the values and power relationships in society. Standard spelling and attitudes to 'correctness' are matters of social as well as linguistic convention.

- **Spelling is CONTEXTUAL.** Spelling and the uses of spelling vary in different contexts.

Understanding these principles and how they operate in language use is an important step towards creating a classroom environment in which children can become efficient language users.

In our society, language learning means learning both oral and written forms. While these two forms of language are clearly very different, it would be wrong to think that learning one form is necessarily exclusive of the other. Consider how much of your oral vocabulary has been learnt from reading. Watch the amount of reading and talk that goes on when children write. The old adages that we learn to read by reading, write by writing and spell by spelling are far too simplistic. While it is accepted that both forms of language are learnt in use, any language learning involves a complex interplay of forms. In order to be a writer it is necessary to be a reader, and spelling relies as much on oral language as it does on reading. This interrelationship is explained by Burke's notion of the 'linguistic data pool' first postulated in 1984 (Harste, Burke & Woodward).

Figure 2: The linguistic data pool

Language is learnt in use. Every encounter we have with language provides an opportunity not only to learn language but to learn *about* language. Our various encounters with language add to our store of knowledge about language – our linguistic data pool. It is this pool of language information, stored in our head, that we call upon in subsequent language encounters. The more language rich our environment, the more encounters we have with language in its various modes, the greater our linguistic data pool.

Learning to write

There are parallels between learning to write and learning to talk. When children begin to talk they do so by babbling. The sounds they make are gradually narrowed to the sounds of the language that surrounds them. These sounds soon become recognisable words and so on. If you observe young children you will find that they begin by what we call *scribbling*. Such scribbling may start by being random, but there is evidence to suggest that it soon becomes culturally specific – it takes on some of the characteristics of print which belong to that culture. (Harste, Burke & Woodward 1984)

INVENTED SPELLING

As children become more attuned to print in the environment, they begin to use letter shapes to represent writing. In many instances these letter shapes are those found in their names. As they begin to read and become aware of the letters of the alphabet they may use single letters or strings of letters to represent writing. These may then become broken into smaller strings to represent individual words. They may then begin to use what has become known as 'invented' spelling (see figure 3).

There is a belief that children should not be encouraged to 'invent' spelling because this leads them into bad habits. If you accept, as we do, that all language is contextual and depends on context for meaning then language learning itself can never be a matter of habit. Moreover, it is in the process of 'inventing' that children learn what English orthography will and will not allow. This is important knowledge when using a dictionary to check

Figure 3: Boats are nice and some boats are speedy

BtS R NIS AD SUMBTS R ZDE.

spelling – you have to know what possible spelling to check. One of the more difficult spelling problems is that of the writer/speller who has no idea of possible alternatives.

RELYING ON SOUND

Children may use one or more of a number of strategies to invent spelling. Phonetic spelling, or spelling as the word sounds, is the most common. This is not surprising, as about 80% of English spelling is phonetically regular.

Spelling as it sounds can involve the writer in exaggerating the sounds in a word so that sounds not normally represented are heard and represented. If you listen carefully as you exaggerate the sounds in the word 'who' you will hear the sound that is made as you release the vowel. It sounds like a 'w' so it is not surprising to find children representing it – 'huw'.

Phonetic spelling is not simply a matter of how words sound. It also involves how those sounds are made, and writers who are uncertain of a spelling will often turn to articulation (the way the sound is made) for a clue. Vowel sounds often cause difficulty, which leads children to rely on this strategy. Vowel sounds are sounds that are made with no impediment to the air stream, as opposed to consonants where such impediment is provided by the lips, teeth, tongue or, as in the case of the nasal sounds, by forcing the air through the nose. Because there is no impediment, the quality of the vowel is very much determined by where in the vocal apparatus the sound is made and by the sounds that occur before and after it. Vowels like 'e' and 'i' are made at the back of the throat while 'o' and 'u', for example, are more fronted. There is an additional complication for the speller. It is often assumed that because we have five letters which represent vowels we have five vowel sounds. This is, in fact, incorrect. English has some twenty-six vowel sounds which are represented by the letters *a, e, i, o* and *u* either used by themselves or in combination with each other and the letters 'r' and 'y'. We also alter the vowel by doubling the final consonant or by adding the so-called silent 'e'.

The system of minimal pairs allows you to work out the vowel sounds if you are so inclined. It also shows up the complications faced in learning vowels. It involves taking words in which there is a single vowel sound and changing that sound. For example:

pat pet pit pot put putt peat port part pate

When you have exhausted one set, try another:

met mat mit meet mate moot etc

(Note that we have already demonstrated two possible representations of the vowel sound in 'peat' and 'meet'. However, 'meat' also occurs, the different spellings of the same word signalling different meanings.)

Faced with such difficulties, children relying on a sound strategy may go to the place of articulation as we have pointed out. In so doing they may settle on one vowel to represent others which are close in place of articulation, for example 'i' and 'e' may simply be represented as 'i'. This strategy may also be applied to consonants close in place of articulation, for example 'tried' becomes 'chrid'. Those wishing to know more about children's phonetic representations should read Charles Read's (1975) seminal study *Children's Categorisation of Speech Sounds in English*. Although this work is now over twenty years old, it is still the basis for our understanding of children's invented spelling.

OTHER STRATEGIES

Other strategies include spelling as it means, as it looks and by analogy. In the first the writer represents semantic units. One of the more common examples is *wasuponatim* – Once upon a time – where the whole semantic unit is represented as one word. The reverse also happens where the writer breaks the word down into perceived semantic units, for example *math you* for Matthew.

The second makes use of visual memory – an important aspect of spelling. However, there is no way of knowing whether a writer is employing this strategy unless there are deviations from the standard. These usually take the form of letter reversals which cannot be explained by the use of other strategies. Some words not related in meaning are spelled according to paradigms, for example *tight, might, right, fright, sight* and so on. If you know how one word is spelled there is a good chance that you can spell the others by analogy.

Developing standard spelling

While it is important to understand that all language learning is integrated, and hence that learning to spell depends on overall language learning, we do need to focus more particularly on spelling if we are to help children to

Figure 4: Spelling strategies

Spelling as it SOUNDS	NASHON – nation, SA – say, FANCE – fancy
Spelling as it SOUNDS OUT	HAFH – half, HUW – who
Spelling as it ARTICULATES	CHRIDAGEN – tried again
Spelling as it MEANS	HAVETO – have to, THANKU – thank you (also as it sounds)
Spelling as it LOOKS	SHCOOL – school, WITHE – white
Spelling by ANALOGY	REALISTICK – realistic, RESKYOU – rescue
Spelling by ALTERNATIVE	You choose a word you can spell or use a letter to place hold that which you are unsure of: eg unsure of vowels the child writes I LIK MI DIL (doll)
Spelling by AUTHORITY	Consult someone. Use a dictionary.

become standard spellers. It is our observation that children have no difficulty learning to spell; they do so in ways that parallel learning to talk. What they have difficulty with is learning the standard spelling. We have often quoted 11-year-old Gilda who, when asked how she would help someone to spell, replied that she did not know: 'Spelling is easy. Getting it right is the hard part.' To us this distinction is important because we would argue that getting it right poses a different learning/teaching problem from that of learning to spell. To put it another way, learning which of the various spellings of a word is the acceptable one is a different learning task from learning the possible alternatives – although they are closely interrelated since standard spelling is one of the possible forms.

It must be emphasised that no two children will develop in exactly the same way. Language and language learning are social activities and the various social groupings in which language learners move are important to their development. Children from families where reading and writing are valued and where children are encouraged to engage in these activities are more likely to develop as readers and writers in ways that ensure success within our education system since our system values such activities. It is likely, although in no way guaranteed, that they will become standard spellers. There are many factors that affect children's learning to read and write, not least the school itself, but it is impossible to account for them all or to explain satisfactorily why some writers fail to become standard spellers even when conditions appear optimal.

While the strategies listed above are important in developing standard spelling, we do not know how they combine. However, it is certain that an over-reliance on a sound-based strategy will not produce a standard speller. When spelling certain words it is clear that one strategy is more likely to lead to standard spelling than another; therefore, children need to be encour- aged to make use of different strategies.

Educators and researchers have not yet come up with the answer to getting it right and perhaps, given the nature of language and social attitudes towards it, they never will. However, there are a number of useful findings which could help us to help learners.

The first is that reading plays an important part in spelling. It is written text that provides demonstrations of standard spelling. Hence, to be a standard speller one must be a reader. A high percentage of spelling problems are, first and foremost, reading problems. However, the ability to read does not guarantee that you will become a standard speller. There are many avid readers who are poor spellers.

Besides being a reader, you must also be a writer. It is when you write that you discover what you need to learn from reading. Many children become reluctant to write because they know they are not standard spellers and this leads to a spiral. They do not write because they cannot use standard spelling but because they do not write they reduce their chances of becoming standard spellers.

Standard spellers, or good spellers as they are commonly called, also have two other characteristics. They can syllabify words and they can break words into their morphemic or meaning components. This is not to say that poor spellers cannot do likewise but it is our observation that they do it less effectively. It is difficult to draw one-on-one correlations between this knowledge and the ability to use standard spelling, but from our observation of young spellers over many years it certainly assists children to become efficient writers and spellers.

Syllabification is important to pronunciation, and pronunciation is important in spelling since a high percentage of English words are phonetic- ally regular. Meaning often accounts for the way we spell words. Knowing the meaning of words and how they are affected by the addition of prefixes and suffixes can help us to spell them. Morphemic knowledge is not the same as finding words within words. *Making, baking* and *taking* are not 'king' words as was suggested by one spelling scheme. They are, in fact, 'ing' words – base words to which 'ing' has been added. To suggest otherwise is to ignore meaning which is the purpose of all language. Knowing the morphemic structure of words involves knowing their meaning. Etymology, the study of the derivation of words is not much in vogue but we have found that an informal study not only helps students to spell but can also be enjoyable at both primary and secondary levels.

While it is possible to isolate some of the characteristics of good spellers, it is not so easy to map the process from invented spelling to standard spelling. The social pressure for standard spelling is so strong that if children do not make the transition of their own accord they must be assisted to do so. However, timing is crucial. When children are starting to write, their concern for spelling does not go beyond simply recording their message, unless they have learnt at a very early age that you cannot write unless you can use standard spelling. Emphasising standard spelling too early in a writer's development inhibits risk-taking and can limit children's development as writers and spellers.

It has been our observation that most children begin to show concern for standard spelling somewhere towards the end of the first year of school. This is not to say that they will not seek the standard spelling prior to this, but by this time they are moving towards a degree of independence in their reading such that they can consciously use it to assist their writing. With or without encouragement they independently display 'have a go' tactics, making several attempts at spelling words they are uncertain of. Children with reading problems may not do this, but by this time they are generally aware of the need for standard spelling even if they are unable to produce it. We believe it is at this point that teaching strategies aimed at encouraging children to proofread should be introduced.

Conditions of learning

How you go about teaching spelling and proofreading very much depends not only on your understanding of spelling but also on what you believe about the way children learn. Many teachers will be familiar with what have become known as Cambourne's 'conditions of learning'. (Cambourne 1984; 1995)

While these conditions provide a useful starting point for thinking about learning, we are increasingly coming to realise that cultural factors play a major part not only in *what* is learnt but in *how* it is learnt. How Cambourne's conditions are realised may vary for different children depending on their cultural background.

Here we explore those conditions of language learning with a particular focus on spelling. None of the conditions described will result in efficient learning on its own. In the spelling classroom it is common to see only a few in place, the one most often neglected being demonstration. All conditions need to be effectively orchestrated for engagement if learning is to take place efficiently.

IMMERSION

In order to learn to be efficient spellers, children need to be in environments where reading and writing are valued and constant activities and where meaningful connections are built between the two.

We live in an environment filled with all kinds of print and a good classroom should reflect this. Books should be readily available and writing should be displayed along with all kinds of other printed materials so that children can scrounge spelling information from a large variety of sources around the room.

Teaching strategies would include modelling, shared book with a spelling focus, shared reading, print walks and an abundance of word games and books.

DEMONSTRATION

Written text provides children with demonstrations of standard spelling. The process of writing helps children to understand the strategies necessary to produce standard spelling. Spelling is, in fact, learnt at the interface between reading and writing. This is one reason why it is important to develop integrated language programs.

The world is full of demonstrations of all kinds so it is important to push to the foreground the particular demonstrations you want your students to learn from. This means that as a teacher you have a very active role in structuring learning. You need to seek ways of ensuring that learning will take place by providing explicit modelling of the skills and processes you want your students to learn.

Teaching strategies would include reading aloud and shared reading with a focus on spelling, making charts for easy access to the demonstrations, modelling daily with explicit demonstrations, and other strategies such as joint construction of text.

ENGAGEMENT

If children are to become standard spellers, it is imperative that they become active readers and writers. They must engage in the demonstrations, and for this to be likely the learning must be perceived by the learner to be meaningful and purposeful.

Because reading provides children with demonstrations of standard spelling, it is extremely difficult, if not impossible, for them to become spellers unless they read. Reading is not enough, however. There are many readers who have problems with spelling. In order to become sensitive to the demonstrations that reading gives, learners have to read like writers, and to do this they must *be* writers.

Teaching strategies must all be purposeful, as this is the key to engagement. The examples of the demonstrations about spelling that can be made through poetry (see chapter 3) are effective in engaging children to explore spelling in an enjoyable and meaningful way.

EXPECTATION

Just as children learn language in an environment where they are expected to succeed, so it is with spelling. Focus on what children can do rather than what they cannot do, and move forward from that point. This does not mean that you ignore deficiencies, but rather adopt a positive, supportive approach, praising what is good and providing help where needed. Expect standard spelling but never allow that expectation to become a barrier to writing.

If learners are in a classroom where there are plenty of messages about how hard spelling is, or how boring learning to spell is, it is most likely they will adopt a similar approach. Spelling and exploring words can be fun and enjoyable. When teaching, think about any hidden messages that your students may be receiving through the language you use, the way you group children and your responses to their efforts.

RESPONSIBILITY

It is important that children come to take responsibility for their own spelling. In the past, teachers took entire responsibility for marking out non-standard spelling. You will need to give considerable help to begin with, but this responsibility should be increasingly passed on to the learner. Learners must come to realise that proofreading is part of the writing process, and they can be taught and supported to engage in this process. Ensure that there are plenty of resources and supports for your learners to take this responsibility.

EMPLOYMENT

Children will only take responsibility for their own spelling if they are given meaningful and purposeful opportunities to write. They will learn to spell only when they have ample opportunities to write in a supportive environment.

When writers perceive that audiences demand standard spelling, they are more likely to develop a concern for it. Therefore they need time to develop their writing, to get their meaning clear and then to proofread.

Teaching strategies would include actually teaching your students to edit and proofread and involving them in lots of activities that require them to apply their knowledge of words.

APPROXIMATION

This is the term used by Cambourne to describe the risk-taking behaviour inherent in all learning. Most learning involves a period of trial and error, evidenced in children's 'invented' spelling. Some teachers and parents worry about allowing children to invent spelling because they believe it encourages them to use non-standard forms. However, invented spelling must be seen within the framework of language learning and the other conditions that apply to it. Rather than hampering children's learning of standard spelling, invented spelling is a necessary part of it.

It is during the trial and error process that students learn the parameters of English spelling: which letter clusters the language allows and does not allow. Without this knowledge, it is doubtful whether we could learn to spell at all, and it is certain that we could not engage in the predictions that enable us to use a dictionary to check spelling.

Teacher modelling of approximating when not certain and how to overcome the spelling problem can provide learners with strategies.

RESPONSE

The crucial role of adult response to children's written communication is implicit in the discussions of the previous conditions. Effective teachers of written language give supportive and constructive responses which focus on how effectively meaning is conveyed. Spelling is part of that effectiveness but it is a means to an end, not an end in itself. The end is the message the child is trying to impart and it should be the principal focus of the response.

Responses that focus primarily on spelling mistakes discourage risk-taking, so that learners write only words which they know how to spell. This invariably leads to dull, uninteresting and unimaginative writing. It is the teacher's role to provide help when children have difficulties. Knowing when and how to respond to children's spelling depends on understanding how we write and the role of spelling in that process. Embedded in this condition is the notion of evaluation, and the adult response contributes to the learner's evaluation of their learning. It is advisable to set up situations such as author's circle whereby learners can get feedback from other students as well as from the teacher.

Beliefs about learning

These conditions do not constitute an explanation for learning itself, and it is outside the scope of this book to offer a theory of learning. However, it is important to share the beliefs about learning which underpin the teaching strategies outlined in the following chapters. These can be summed up as follows:

- Learning is to the brain what breathing is to the lungs. We are learning all the time. What children learn may not necessarily be what teachers teach.

- Children are more likely to learn when what they learn is meaningful and has purpose.

- Since meaning resides in the total language context, whole to part learning is more meaningful than part to whole.

- Knowledge is constructed by the learner through interaction with the social and physical environment. Learning is, therefore, a multi-layered social activity.

Within this framework, spelling is best learnt through reading and writing. While there is no guarantee that children will become standard spellers, they are more likely to do so if they have opportunities to write for real purposes, for audiences that demand standard spelling, and if they are given opportunities to explore possible spellings for themselves.

While much of our language learning is incidental, it is equally true that much of our conscious knowledge about language is learnt more formally. We believe there is a place in language learning for formal teaching. For us, *demonstration* encompasses such teaching. The difficult questions of what should be the content of such teaching, in what circumstances it is appropriate, and how it should be done can only be answered in terms of each individual learner and the circumstances pertaining at the time. For those who argue for direct sequenced teaching this appears laissez faire, but it is far from it. The logic by which we learn is not the logic often imposed by teaching schemes. Being able to respond to learners at the point of need requires a teacher who understands learners and language and who can create a variety of learning environments. Creating the need for learning, the conditions in which it can take place, and the demonstrations that are necessary is what teaching is about.

2

Teaching spelling

How do we teach spelling?

During the 1970s there was a great deal research into the effectiveness of traditional spelling programs by a variety of researchers such as Callaway, McDaniel and Mason (1972), Beers (1977) and Hammill (1977) to name a few. Studies by Hammill, Larsen and McNutt (1977) suggested that students with no formal spelling instruction but who had a good deal of reading and writing instruction could spell as well as their peers. Read's study (1975) and that of Bissex (1980) provided important insights into children's so-called invented spelling and its relationship to spelling development. The identification of the spelling strategies that learners and effective spellers use (Bouffler 1984) also suggested useful teaching strategies. However, while the teaching of reading and writing underwent considerable change in the 1980s, the teaching of spelling remained separate and traditional. Since complaints about children's spelling have long been with us, perhaps it is time to consider that change might be necessary in our approach to teaching.

Our own research suggests that an integrated approach is likely to be more effective than stand-alone activities. Of course aspects of previous approaches will find a place in any good language program but these need to be taught in an integrated and more meaningful way as part of reading and writing. The following factors should be considered when developing a well-balanced program that will lead to more successful teaching and learning of spelling.

1. SPELLING IS A COMPLEX PROCESS

With approaches such as memorisation of lists or simply writing to learn to spell, we are not acknowledging the complex nature of the spelling process.

Spelling is not just a memorisation process; it is acquired and learned as part of writing and reading.

Sounding out is a commonly used strategy but there are nine other strategies available. It would be impossible to know and list all the rules that would be needed to describe the letter–sound correspondences in English but put simply, letters are what you see and sounds are what you hear. A consistent way to talk about letters is by the letter name not sound.

In addition, the debates that continue are sometimes made confusing by the misuse of terms.

> To understand phonics, we need to understand phonology and orthography, since phonics refers to the complex relationships between these two systems.
> *Phonology* (or phonemics) is the study of the sound system of a language.
> *Phonemics* is the study of classes of sounds that constitute significant differences in a language. We have 46 phonemes in English.
> *Orthography* refers to the written symbols of a language.
> *Phonemic awareness* is the awareness of sounds in words.
> *Phonetics* deals with the characteristics of speech sounds and how they are produced.
> (Adapted from *Practically Primary*, June 1996)

2. SPELLING IS A DEVELOPMENTAL PROCESS

Observation over time of several pieces of any student's writing will reveal spelling development. Since not every child will learn in exactly the same way, there will be differences in the way individual learners learn their spelling. There is no evidence that each child will learn through specific stages in exactly the same way. The choice of teaching strategies will depend on the child's development as a reader and writer.

3. SPELLING SHOULD BE INTEGRATED

Spelling activities should be a natural consequence of reading and writing. Literature and the student's own writing provide opportunities for learning about spelling. When spelling is taught in this way, the emphasis is on meaning and effective communication, not on spelling for spelling's sake. A focus on spelling can take place across all learning areas in addition to specific time that may be set aside when required.

4. SPELLING SHOULD OCCUR IN CONTEXT

Learning to spell involves being able to recognise non-standard forms in text. It is important that teaching always focuses on words in text, not words in isolation.

5. WRITING SHOULD HAVE AUDIENCE AND PURPOSE

If children are to become good writers, and that includes good spellers, they must have reasons for doing so. A balanced literacy classroom is one that provides real purposes for writing. Research (Bouffler 1984) shows that when these contexts include audiences that demand standard spelling, children will take greater care with their spelling and will be more concerned with standard forms. Integral to developing good spellers is providing writing experiences with real purposes that are obvious and meaningful to the learner.

6. INVENTED SPELLING IS AN OPPORTUNITY FOR LEARNING

Risk-taking behaviour is evidenced in children's so-called invented spelling. Surprisingly perhaps, invented spelling is not just a learning strategy used by children. The 'have-a-go' approach is used by all writers when they don't know the spelling of a word. The use of invented or 'temporary' spelling by beginning writers is a useful assessment tool for observing the learning strategies in use. It is during the trial-and-error process that children learn the parameters of the English language: which letter clusters the language allows and does not allow. Without this knowledge, it is doubtful if we could learn to spell at all and it is certain that we could not engage in those predictions that enable us to use a dictionary to check spelling.

7. EDITING AND PROOFREADING ARE SPECIFIC SKILLS THAT MUST BE TAUGHT

When audience and purpose demand it, proofreading is an important part of the writing process. Since the purpose of proofreading is to ensure that the surface features of text are standard, spelling and proofreading are inextricably linked. 'Getting it right' is not easy, even for proficient writers, and children need considerable help to learn these skills. Proofreading and editing skills must be explicitly taught.

8. TEXT IS AN OPPORTUNITY FOR LEARNING SPELLING

All written texts, especially literature, provide demonstrations of standard spelling and punctuation. Therefore, they are a source of teaching about spelling. Even non-standard text can be used, especially in the teaching of proofreading.

The role of the teacher and the learner

The development of any program is linked with teacher beliefs about how language is learned. Implicit in an integrated approach is a belief that students must be assisted and encouraged to develop some responsibility for their own learning. As teachers, we put the structures and learning experiences in place, but ultimately it is the student who must do the learning.

Students can only take that control of their learning when they have the knowledge and experience to make the necessary decisions. To state the obvious, learners fail when the task is beyond them. When you pick up a piece of writing which has so much wrong with it that you do not know where to begin to help the learner, then it is most likely that you are looking at a learner who is not getting sufficient support. We must always ensure that the student has enough control over the elements of the particular writing task to ensure some degree of success.

Some of the strategies that follow may appear in some instances to restrict the learner's writing by constraining topic choice or the kind of text written. On the contrary, the strategies, when used appropriately in a balanced program, will place control with the learner because they narrow the focus and make the learning task manageable. The teacher's role is clearly one of assessing learners and orchestrating learning situations which will progressively lead to greater and greater learner control of language. Since only teachers know the needs of their classes, only teachers can design learning programs for those classes. The teaching strategies that follow are not a language program but, rather, tools to help the design of language programs that integrate spelling.

The environment

In order to create a learning environment, we have to provide supports and scaffolds so that children can be risk-takers and can assume responsibility for their own learning. There are a variety of things that we can do for this to happen in spelling, particularly in the early school years of schooling. Some will be fairly obvious; nevertheless, they are worth restating.

CLASSROOM PRINT

Print in the classroom must be accessible. This means print at the right height for children to read. Colourful displays high on the walls and ceilings create an attractive learning environment but do not provide a support for children learning to spell. They need print they can use, print they can see, and lists of words on display that are meaningful such as labels. They need print that is changing all the time.

ALPHABET STRIPS

Early classrooms should have a large alphabet strip that is referred to often when reading and playing with words. It too should be at an accessible height. Many children will also benefit from a personal alphabet strip on their desk. If arranged in a strip where children can run their fingers beneath the letters, it is much easier for young writers. It is also of benefit to have a variety of letter books and student-made alphabet books. Letter names are the best place to start, not sounds, simply because letter names are consistent and sounds are not. As sounds are introduced in meaningful contexts, children will come to understand that one letter may represent a number of sounds.

LETTER MANIPULATION

Opportunities to play with, feel and manipulate letters are essential for young writers. Magnetic letters are ideal for matching and sorting in any number of ways. Opportunities for writing in sand or with paint, or cutting out and using sandpaper or felt letters are very worthwhile for beginning writers because they learn how to discriminate between letters quickly.

> What we have overlooked for too long is the fact that before a child can attach a sound to a letter symbol he has first of all to be able to see the letter symbol as an individual entity different from other symbols. (Clay 1991, p. 266)

BOOKS

Provide a variety of easily accessible texts. Individual book boxes containing books appropriate to the children's reading level and interest are ideal. In addition, a class library is essential. The library should be welcoming, regularly changing and should contain a variety of texts: stories, poems and factual texts. Take time to introduce children to the books in the class library. If they know what is there they can use the books to greater benefit. Demonstrations and use of books in the early stages should be for enjoyment but also seen as an opportunity to demonstrate concepts about print and spelling.

WRITING OPPORTUNITIES

Lots of opportunities to write a variety of texts and, particularly, to create class books on everyday topics, not only demonstrate a purpose for writing but will help to expand the reading materials in the classroom. This is particularly so at the very early stages where lots and lots of books with familiar text are required. Surrounding learners with all kinds of print that they have contributed to or that has grown out of a shared activity helps to reinforce the varied purposes for writing and reading.

GAMES

Games are essentially about having fun, but we can also learn from them. If there are lots of activities that are about having fun with words, the classroom will be a place where spelling is looked upon very positively. While there is no substitute for reading a book, there will be many occasions when children will enjoy playing with words with games like I Spy and Bingo. Finding letters in news stories, words that sound the same, or words that sound the same but look different are fun ways of directing children's attention to the print around them. Crosswords are another favourite word-based game. Have children create their own crosswords, find hidden words and engage in the wide variety of word-based games.

OTHER RESOURCES

The environment created in a classroom to encourage language development and enjoyment of learning must contain all the supports students will require as they continue to learn. Dictionaries vary a great deal and must be selected carefully to meet students' needs. For older classes there are etymological dictionaries, books which give the history of words, and dictionaries of idioms, proverbs and eponyms which students enjoy browsing through. A selection of thesauruses is also a valuable classroom resource.

Guiding principles

DAILY WRITING

Opportunities to read and write on a daily basis are crucial. The classroom should be a place where these things are important, and where they are seen as not only enjoyable activities but purposeful activities. Lots of meaningful contexts need to be created where children can write for a variety of genuine audiences.

For many children this is an encouragement to engage in the processes involved in writing. For beginning writers, it will be during the writing process that the 'sound' of words will gain importance. You will be able to observe children sounding out the words they want to use, as well as using the alphabet strips on their desk. It is important to observe closely how effective this strategy is for your young writers and to determine whether they need more or less sounding out to proceed without frustration at these very early stages.

HAVE A GO

Some students need encouragement to take risks and to learn that they need not get it 'right' the first time. Introducing the 'have a go' card can help to demonstrate that you may need more than one go at getting it right. The language we use to help children understand this is important. It does not mean that anything will do and that eventually we will either tell them the answer or simply leave it without comment. Rather, it is a strategy to teach children to make an effort, to deeply consider how a word might be spelt. Being able to generate alternative spellings for a word is a crucial strategy which will remain useful right through life.

LOOK/COVER/WRITE/CHECK

For many children this is an efficient way of learning words, particularly those words that they are having difficulty with, although it would be painstaking as the only strategy. It is really just sophisticated memorisation, and will assist some children by giving them the opportunity to focus on an irregular word and commit it to memory. For many of your students you will observe that the visual strategy is not enough and that for them you may need to discuss the word and put it in a context, for example, as well as asking them to memorise it. Sadler (1981) expanded this strategy to 'look, say, cover, write, check'.

MODELLING

Modelling writing and talking through the process as you write in front of the class and/or group is invaluable for all learners. Many children may never actually have seen a writer writing and therefore may have developed some very confusing beliefs about writing and spelling. Modelling writing, and making a focus of spelling particular words appropriate to the group you are modelling for, should be a regular activity.

TALK

As with modelling, opportunities to talk about writing experiences, what children are writing and how they are going about their writing is invaluable. This can take many forms from informally working with a partner through to the use of the author's circle.

REAL PURPOSES AND AUDIENCES

Creating real purposes and audiences for writing from day one is one of the single most important things we can do if we want our writers to work towards using correct spelling. Without knowing who they are writing for and why, they will have little reason to engage in the process and attend to the surface features of their writing. As they develop a real understanding about the social nature of writing they will become more aware of the notion of audience and purpose. If we know this is important we must tell our students. We need to work hard at creating real contexts for writing beyond the classroom.

PERSONAL DICTIONARIES

Many beginning writers will find the development of a personal dictionary useful. This involves recording words alphabetically, most probably after identifying the words in their writing during a conference with the teacher. It may be a word that you have identified in a particular piece of writing, it may be a word from a whole-class activity that you have decided will be useful for all children to have in their dictionaries. There are a couple of points to note here. Firstly, the dictionaries need checking and the words entered must be spelt correctly if this is to be a useful resource for the writer. Secondly, if it is a dictionary the word should have a definition beside it, otherwise it will be a personal word list.

GIVE STUDENTS REAL RESPONSES

Writing for most young children is physically quite tiring. They may have much to say but the actual task of handwriting and struggling with spelling in the beginning makes writing hard work for many. Given the importance of the task and the likelihood that you wish to make it pleasurable and meaningful, children need responses to their writing. This means you need to respond to the meaning on the page. For many young writers a tick or a 'good work' is unlikely to be a just reward for the effort they are making. They need to know that they have an audience and that they are communicating with that audience, and in the first instance this is likely to be the teacher. Your role is crucial, albeit time consuming, and involves responding regularly in a meaningful way.

EMPHASISE AUDIENCE

Author's circle is a way of introducing children to the notion of an audience for their writing. For this strategy to be useful, children must learn to take turns and listen to each other. They will learn how to give each other feedback from the example that you set, so you need to be conscious of the demonstrations that you give. Five children in a group is an ideal number, each with a piece of writing which is incomplete, or completed only to draft stage, otherwise the writer will not be receptive. Each child has an opportunity to read their piece and be questioned by, or to ask questions of, each member of the group. They will need some help to ask questions about meaning, something that they perhaps did not understand, something that the writer may have left out. It is quite a skill to listen carefully and to ask a question about what is heard and so this is a strategy that develops over time.

PERSONAL WRITING FOLDERS

If we want children to engage in the process of writing, the best organisation is a writing folder in which they can store loose pieces of paper. The folder is added to as required and various drafts stapled or clipped together. The use of a book for draft writing seems to contradict the process. The very fact that it is a book inhibits children from crossing out and making changes. It can put pressure on some children to get it right the first time and in so doing inhibit the quality of their writing.

We have to consider the hidden messages we give children in all the actions we take. As we assess and evaluate the methods and strategies in use we should be continually modifying what we are doing in the classroom. Finally, be clear about the language you use; what are referred to here are writing folders, not story-writing folders.

THE WRITING PROCESS

Use every opportunity to talk about the writing process. Comment on the author's craft when reading, make a point about something you noticed after silent reading, and utilise all opportunities. Be explicit about the writing process before specific writing times in the classroom. Charts that remind children about what to do when they have finished the first draft, how to prepare for publication, and what to look for in their writing can be helpful. Charts demonstrating the process need to be appropriate to meet the needs of each writer and could take the form of a checklist which is continually added to during the writing conference. This could be stored in the writing folder.

USING POETRY

Demonstrations of language at work are plentiful in poetry and so this particular genre provides a wonderful vehicle for focusing on words in context. Focusing on particular words should follow enjoyment of the poem. Focus activities may involve a list of words that sound the same as the one taken from the text or finding words that mean the same as the one taken from the text. When appropriate, your young spellers will need to learn more about words in order to build the lists and ensure a continued interest in words. The result of activities such as identifying the rhyme in words like *frock, lock, rock, sock* is the knowledge each child develops about spelling. They not only have the poetry they have engaged with but the lists that have been developed, and are continuing to develop, can be displayed in the room. Having children use a notebook for recording words 'discovered' in these demonstrations means that the words are available for students should they wish to check spelling in the future.

SHARED READING

When texts are chosen for their literary value for shared book experience, many opportunities exist to make demonstrations relating to spelling and punctuation in ongoing readings of the text. Because these demonstrations are made in the context of a familiar text, these demonstrations are very powerful. The demonstrations made can be planned to meet the needs of a particular group or for a whole class. The shared book experience can be used with a variety of text types. For example Roald Dahl's *The BFG* is a great source of language demonstrations. At one point the BFG refers to giants as being 'murderful'. This may well be a jumping off point for a discussion on the suffix '-ful'. Do we say *murderful*? Why? Why not?

GUIDED READING

These group sessions, where every child has a copy of the text in a small group situation, can provide opportunities to make demonstrations about words or punctuation on the spot. Given that texts will be appropriate and carefully chosen for the reading task, they should be ideal for these purposes. Small whiteboards are useful for making these demonstrations quickly and visibly to the group.

SPELL CHECKS

Students are getting more and more opportunities to compose their writing on computers both in the classroom and at home. They can easily access spell checks which are useful, particularly for typing errors. Where the errors are genuinely spelling errors they will still need to be able to select the correct spelling. In most cases the spell check on the computer identifies the word out of context and the young writer needs to understand that they have to consider the spelling of the word within the context of the writing.

3

Teaching and learning strategies for reading, writing and spelling

The following strategies incorporate both reading and writing. Their main focus is the development of writing and, within that, the development of standard spelling. This focus supports an integrated approach that views spelling as an aspect of reading and writing. This does not mean that your students will learn to spell by accident if they are reading and writing. The program you put in place has to be well planned and thoroughly thought through so that very specific demonstrations about spelling can be made through your reading and writing program which must, in turn, be structured to allow this to happen.

At the same time, teachers must be flexible enough to respond to those 'teachable moments' that often present themselves. Words, their spelling and their meanings will be constantly a focus throughout the day and in all key learning areas in any classroom where spelling is taught in context. These strategies provide a way of making such links.

Some of the procedures outlined focus on writing and are aimed at helping learners gain control over various aspects of the writing process, since control over the process has implications for control over spelling. The reading strategies are aimed at supporting aspects of the writing process as well as developing reading skills. The more students learn about text through reading, the more they will learn about creating text. The strategies are designed to supplement other literature-based reading activities. They are not sufficient to constitute the reading component of an integrated language program.

The teaching strategies fall broadly into the following categories:

    1. Strategies to encourage writing and risk-taking

    2. Strategies to sensitise language learners to words in context

    3. Strategies to develop proofreading (chapter 4)

While these strategies may at first seem unrelated to spelling, we would argue that this is not so. To be a speller you need to be a reader and a writer. 'Written conversation', 'Dialogue journals' and 'Modelling' are all aimed at getting children to write. Within each of these strategies there will be opportunities for teachers to model standard spelling in their responses, or talk about aspects of spelling once a text has been modelled. Depending on the grade, modelling a text should include also include modelling editing and proofreading.

    'Story schema', 'Text schema', 'Bundling' and 'Big cloze' are examples of strategies that are aimed at extending students' writing through a developing knowledge of how text is constructed. Once they are comfortable with writing, spelling can be dealt with through proofreading and other text-related strategies. We would emphasise that these strategies are not exhaustive.

    Although students often see editing and proofreading as simply involving spelling, clearly this is not so. Therefore Chapter 4 contains two strategies, 'Think me a poem' and 'Who said', that draw attention firstly to what editing is about and secondly to punctuation, another important aspect of proof-reading.

Strategies to encourage writing and risk-taking

WRITTEN CONVERSATION

Focus: *writing/spelling*

Rationale

This strategy is a conversation on paper. It enables children to make use of their knowledge of oral language and the nature of conversation and apply it to writing. It is one procedure where the emphasis is on the message and not on the surface features of the writing, allowing learners to take risks in a supportive and non-threatening environment. It is predicated on the belief that when we use language we learn about language and what we learn in one language situation we can apply to another.

Grouping

Pairs, either individual child and teacher or children in pairs.

Materials

Pen and paper.

Procedure

Two participants converse on paper. Where the learner has reading difficulties the partner may need to read what has been written.

The art of this strategy lies in being a good conversationalist, and asking questions that will demand more than a simple one-word answer. Some children will require help to get their message on paper, and the type of help will depend on the needs of the particular child. It will be an opportunity to direct the child to language strategies they might use in order to solve their spelling problems. Where appropriate ask:

Figure 5: Example of a teacher/learner written conversation

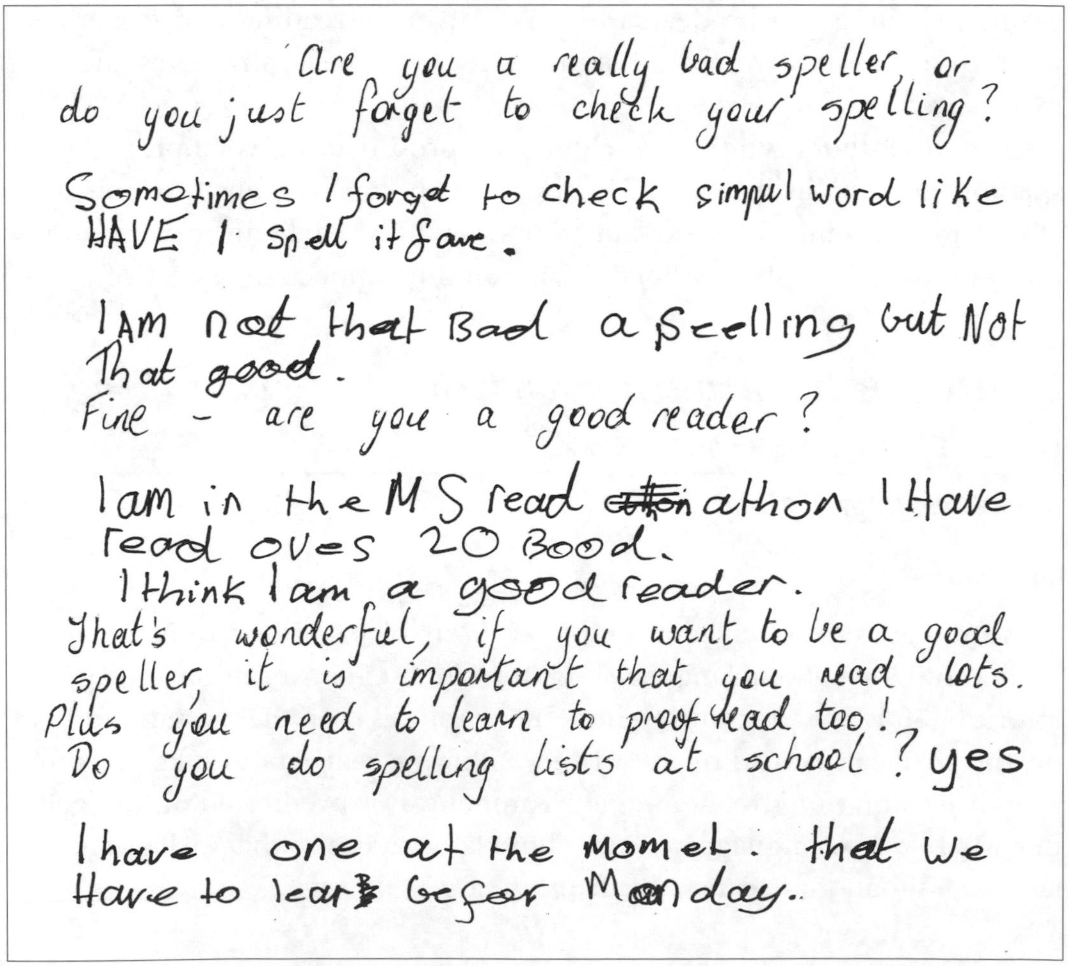

Are you a really bad speller, or do you just forget to check your spelling?

Sometimes I forgot to check simpul word like HAVE I spell it fave.

I AM not that Bad a Scelling but Not That good.

Fine – are you a good reader?

I am in the MS read athon I Have read oves 20 Bood. I think I am a good reader.

That's wonderful, if you want to be a good speller, it is important that you read lots. Plus you need to learn to proof read too! Do you do spelling lists at school? yes

I have one at the momel. that We Have to lear Gefor Monday.

What sounds do you hear?

Where have you seen the word before?

Can you find that word in the room?

What other words do you know that are similar?

As a stimulus for reluctant writers, Written Conversation is also effective as a group or whole-class activity where children converse in pairs. In this case they rely on each other for assistance, which will be a consideration when allocating pairs. Written Conversation on a teacher–learner basis is a labour-intensive procedure, best used for children who have been identified as needing help to become risk-takers in their writing.

DIALOGUE JOURNALS

Focus: *writing/spelling*

Rationale

This strategy enables learners to use their knowledge of oral language and the feedback provided by the dialogue, and to apply it to writing. The emphasis is on the message and not on the surface features of the language, so learners can take risks with their writing in a non-threatening situation. The response enables learners to judge the success of their communication and provides opportunities for the teacher, or respondent, to model standard forms of language. This procedure is a logical extension of Written Conversation. With Dialogue Journals, however, distance from the audience is increased and the meaning must be able to be sustained over time.

Grouping

This procedure best operates on a learner/teacher basis. Once teachers become confident with it, it is no more time consuming than the marking of written work and provides a great deal of information about the student's control of writing and spelling.

Materials

An exercise book or similar.

Procedure

There are many ways to set up a dialogue. One is to have the learner choose an important person, place or thing and to tell you something about it. You then respond by focusing on the communication and sharing something of interest with the learner, and so the process continues. The frequency of the dialogue will depend largely on the nature and magnitude of the learning problem being addressed. For children who are reluctant writers, it may be necessary to concentrate solely on this kind of writing for a period of time and on a daily basis. These journals can be extremely successful and lead to the development of excellent teacher/student relationships. Because of their highly personal nature, they should be treated sensitively and privacy should be honoured. Learners may well share things in confidence and that confidence needs to be respected.

MODELLING

Focus: *reading/writing/spelling*

Rationale

A good language-learning environment is one that provides regular demonstrations of language in use. Most teachers appreciate the benefits of reading to and with their classes, and modelling writing behaviours is equally as important. Through their reading, children see the product of the writing process but they may not often see the process in action. Modelled writing involves the teacher composing in front of the class, thinking aloud about what is being done as it is being done, and explaining why it is being done. This experience enables young writers to understand how writers go about writing, how conventions are used, and how different kinds of texts are structured.

Modelling the process is important for developing writers, as is modelling the product. When writers are faced with a writing task they do not know how to complete, they may improvise on what they do know how to write, or find examples of how other writers have tackled the task.

Grouping

Small group or whole class

Materials

Blackboard and chalk, butcher's paper and large felt pen, or overhead.

Procedure

The procedure will depend on the particular demonstration that you have determined is appropriate for the group. During modelling, the teacher may demonstrate any number of things concerned with text and how it works, including:

- conventions – spelling, grammar and punctuation
- using environmental print to locate the spelling of a word
- using resources
- modelling spelling strategies considered appropriate to the group (see figure 4)
- how different types of text are structured – narrative, report, poem, letter
- how to begin a piece of writing appropriate to the text type
- how to organise information: sequencing and logical development
- adding detail
- ways of saying the same thing (style)
- editing devices

Modelling is based in some ways on the writing abilities of the teacher and the appropriateness of the modelling done to meet the needs of the group. Children can be called on to help solve problems and this will be more effective if the situation is meaningful. They will learn that writers often 'struggle' with their writing and have to work hard at drafting and redrafting a piece of text. If beginning writers never see a writer writing, they may develop false ideas about the writing process, even in supportive classrooms.

MODELLING TEXT

Other writers can also serve as models for structuring text, providing another kind of modelling. Children will have difficulty writing narrative if they do not read narrative, poems unless they read poems and so on. The same is true of factual texts. With young writers, this kind of modelling may take the form of retelling a story or in the creative improvisation of a story, particularly making use of the story structure rather than the content. Modelling in this way can help them to begin to read like writers. It can also be used to support writers in difficulty, particularly the non risk-takers, by having them improvise on highly predictable texts. All texts are more or less predictable but highly predictable texts tend to exploit such things as accumulation, repetition and rhyme, signalling changes in text by appropriate illustrations. Texts such as the traditional *I Know an Old Lady Who Swallowed a Fly* which uses rhyme and accumulation, or *Brown Bear, Brown Bear* and *Polar Bear, Polar Bear* which use repetition, are examples of predictable texts. Using texts like these as models, children can write their own versions.

DEVELOPING NARRATIVE

As children begin to gain control of the writing process, they move from recount to narrative. Many texts that are often called narratives are not narratives in the true sense. Young writers often write observations and comments and call them stories. Coming to grips with the narrative structure may require a little help. First and foremost, this will come from reading. When discussing writing and particular writing tasks with children, we need to pay attention to the language we use. Even now, with the emphasis on text types, it is still not unusual to find young children with 'story-writing' folders or books. We maintain that this can be very confusing for many young writers.

The following procedures are useful for helping children to write narrative. The purposes and types of texts presuppose particular audiences which range from self, to close friends and associates, to impersonal audiences. Traditionally, the most common audience for a student's writing has been the class teacher and perhaps their peers. While these are legitimate, audiences need to go beyond the classroom if the children are to understand the importance of standard spelling and use it consistently.

PICTURE WRITING

Focus: *writing*

Rationale

All narratives have a setting and some characters, and manipulating both is often difficult in the early stages. By providing learners with a setting, in the form of a picture, and encouraging them to create the characters which might belong to that setting, you can assist the learner to discover a focus for narrative writing. The very process of creating characters and relating them to a setting prompts narrative. Drawing characters provides rehearsal and focus.

This strategy gives a purpose for writing, and provides the student with an opportunity to engage in the process of writing and to practise developing spelling skills.

Grouping

Individual, cooperative pairs.

Materials

Pen, scissors and paste, a collection of pictures showing various settings.

Procedure

Allow the writer to choose a picture and ask them to create and draw some characters that might go with it. Have them cut out the characters and attach them to the picture. Then have the writer write a story using the picture and the characters.

STORY SCHEMA

Focus: *reading/writing*

Rationale

Since narrative has a clearly defined structure, writing narrative involves the control of that structure. At a global level, the structure may be defined as orientation, complication and resolution. More specifically, however, a narrative is composed of a number of transition points around which shifts in plot and theme occur. To the reader, these transition points are major points of prediction. Getting readers to focus on such transition points will develop their understanding of narrative structure and assist them in their reading and writing.

Engaging in the reading process using this strategy will provide the opportunity for the teacher to make demonstrations about words in context.

Grouping

Whole class or group.

Materials

Familiar stories cut at transition points so that each learner will have a piece of the story.

Procedure

Shuffle the story pieces and distribute them among the class or group. Tell children that they each have a piece of a story that they are going to try to put back together. Ask:

Who has the beginning?
How do you know you have the beginning? (Ask the learner to read).
Who has the next bit?
Why do you think it is the next bit? (The learners reads the next bit and so on until the story is reconstructed.)

FACTUAL TEXT

While narrative structure is fairly familiar to most of us, factual texts vary in their structure depending on their type and purpose. A report obviously differs from a factual description or an argument, but at the same time it is possible that a report may contain description and argument. What becomes obvious is the close relationship between language and thinking. Developing factual text means developing the thinking processes of classification, generalisation, explanation, and cause and effect. Modelling is an appropriate procedure to use with factual texts as well as narrative.

TEXT SCHEMA

Focus: *reading/writing*

Rationale

This is a similar procedure to story schema. Non-narrative also has clearly defined transition points which are major points for prediction. Focusing on these can help learners to understand the structure of texts and provides models of text types for their own writing.

Grouping

Small group or individual.

Materials

Non-narrative text cut at transition points.

Procedure

Give each group/individual all the pieces of the text and ask them to reassemble them. There may be alternative ways of doing this. Where alternatives make sense they should be discussed and accepted. Ask children to justify their ordering. Because non-narrative text may vary in its general structure, readers need all the pieces in front of them to complete the task.

BUNDLING

Focus: *writing/spelling*

Rationale

How text is structured depends on the writer's purpose and the information to be conveyed, and this determines the type of text. Organising and sequencing information can help writers to structure text, and helps them to plan their writing. Children should be encouraged to use a variety of strategies to check and correct unfamiliar spelling at the planning stage.

Grouping

Individual or group.

Materials

A supply of small cards cut into uniform size.

Procedure

Have children jot down all they know about their chosen and/or researched topic using a card for each separate piece of information. They should then spread the cards in front of them. Then help them to select the main ideas from the cards and group or 'bundle' the remaining cards under the main ideas. These become the supporting facts. With simple reports, the cards can be first assembled under *who, when* and *what* and then reassembled. If information is missing it becomes obvious. No cards supporting a main idea may suggest a lack of information or supporting evidence. Help children by asking: *Are there sufficient main ideas or is there a need for more research?* The organisation can be used as a flexible basis for writing. Information can be added, omitted or reorganised during writing but the bundles provide a focus to support the learner during writing. This procedure also provides an excellent introduction to paragraphing.

Figure 6: 'Cards' from a bundling activity

* KARATE *

Karate is for self-defence.	There are different styles of Karate.	We wear white suits called 'Gis'.	You begin the lesson by bowing to the founder of Karate, Masoyama.
		You tie your Gi with a coloured belt.	
?	?	You start with a white-belt.	Lessons consist of warm-ups, we do star-jumps & stretching and running.
		Black is the highest belt.	We work on our moves & positions.
		To go from one level to another, you have to pass a grading.	

BIG CLOZE

Focus: *reading/writing/spelling*

Rationale

When writing informational text, the writer is required to explain, substantiate assertions and draw conclusions. Cause and effect relationships are signalled linguistically by the use if words such as 'because', 'so' and 'therefore'.

Grouping

Individual or small group.

Materials

Texts which include an explanation. Delete either the cause or effect to create a big cloze. See figure 7 for an example.

Procedure

Have children complete the cloze by creating appropriate text for each gap. This can be done individually or cooperatively. There is no one right answer. Any completion that fits within the meaning of the total text should be accepted. Children should be encouraged to justify and discuss completions. The post-cloze discussion is the most important part of the activity, not only to examine final sentence structure but to attend to spelling and punctuation in the context of the text.

Strategies to sensitise language learners to words in context

Since language is used to make meaning, any activity which focuses on words must focus on meaning. Understanding the range of meanings that words can have is crucial to spelling. This includes understanding their morphemic structure, or how they are made up.

The following strategies focus on words in context and, while meaning is the prime concern, they provide opportunities for further demonstrations and discussions about morphemic structure and spelling. A discussion on word structure and spelling should always follow on from the strategies to make full use of the experience.

Figure 7: Example of a big cloze text

The Birthday Party

It was Janet's birthday on Saturday and she decided it would be fun to have a

small party. This was Monday so_____

_____.

Her room was small and she had few plates and glasses so_____

_____

_____.

She decided to invite Karen, Michael, Rosemary, John, Stephen, Jane and

Chris. When she rang Karen she got the answering machine because _____

_____

so_____.

He was at home and agreed to come but _____

_____.

His friend was an exchange student from Japan who was staying with him.

Therefore_____

_____. Because_____

_____

It was easy to contact Rosemary and John. Stephen was away at camp. Jane

and Chris were also glad to come and with Michael's friend Koji there would

still be eight. Because_____

_____she planned to go

shopping on Thursday evening.

WRITTEN CLOZE

Focus: *reading/writing/spelling*

Rationale

Reading is a process of sampling print, predicting meaning and confirming on the basis of further sampling. When we predict, we make use of the three cuing systems of language: the syntactic system, the semantic system and the graphophonic system. When readers are required to complete word gaps in text, they make use of all these systems. By controlling the deletions, it is possible to force the reader to focus more heavily on one or other of the cuing systems. Written completion also provides the opportunity to discuss questions of spelling as well as the appropriateness of the word chosen to fill the gap.

Grouping

Individual or small group.

Materials

Text with appropriate deletions. See figure 8 for an example.

Procedure

A standard cloze involves selecting a passage, leaving the first one or two sentences intact, and then deleting words at regular intervals (usually about 1 in 10). Controlled cloze involves deleting either semantic, grammatical or sound/symbol elements only, which means that the deletion rate may vary, but the first few sentences should still be left intact to provide an entry to the text. If the controlled cloze is designed for discussion of spelling, the deletions would focus on the words for the discussion.

Have children complete the passage. This can be done cooperatively or individually. Discuss the fillers. Do they make sense? Accept any meaningful filler. Allow children to compare their versions with the original. Ask them to check the spelling of words used to fill the gaps. Follow up this activity with a discussion about the words. Design cloze activities that focus on the particular needs of the student. This could include:

- sound/symbol relationships
- word endings
- beginning sounds
- vowels
- words that sound the same but have different spelling
- silent letters

Figure 8: Example of a written cloze text

Once, long ago, there lived a man who was blessed with a fine house, healthy

animals and fertile land. This man was also lucky enough to have a_____,

loving son, but the boy had never known_____but good times.

'The lad must learn to_____with ill-luck,' said his father.

From then on he gave his_____all the awkward jobs. However, luck

was with the boy_____the day his father sent him into

the_____to bring back timber. Only a rickety cart was free for the

and the_____ father watched the son harness two oxen to the

_____.'If that cart breaks up today, then it will be a good

for the boy,' he thought.

The_____smiled at his son. 'If that cart_____up when you are

alone in the forest, necessity will_____you what to do,' he said.

Adapted from 'The Best Teacher' in B. Hayes & R. Ingpen, *Folk Tales and Fables of the World*, Reader's Digest, Sydney, 1989.

SYNONYM SUBSTITUTION

Focus: *reading/spelling*

Rationale

Reading involves prediction. When readers predict, they make use of the three cuing systems of language. However, correspondence between what is written and what is read is not always exact, and readers may vary the text and still maintain meaning. While readers do not necessarily read exactly what is written, writers deliberately choose particular words to convey their meaning. By focusing on substitutions and the original word, or words, it is possible to examine nuances of meaning. Understanding meaning is crucial to spelling. This procedure also provides ample opportunities to focus on spelling by looking at words in context. As well, it provides an authentic situation to use classroom resources such as dictionaries and thesauruses to explore words and their meanings.

Figure 9: Examples of a text for synonym substitution

The Three Little Pigs

Once upon a time there were three <u>little</u> pigs. They lived with their mother.

One day the mother pig said, '<u>Little</u> pigs you are <u>big</u> now. You must find your own <u>houses</u>.' So off went the three little pigs to build their own <u>houses</u>.

The first <u>little</u> pig found some <u>straw</u> so he built his <u>house</u> of <u>straw</u>.

The second <u>little</u> pig found some <u>sticks</u>, so he built his <u>house</u> of <u>sticks</u>.

The third <u>little</u> pig wanted a strong house, so he built his <u>house</u> of <u>bricks</u>.

One day the first <u>little</u> pig was <u>making</u> his dinner, when he heard a knock at the door. He peeped out the window and saw the <u>big</u> bad wolf. '<u>Little</u> pig, <u>little</u> pig, let me in,' said the wolf.

'No! No! not by the <u>hair</u> on my chinny chin chin,' cried the first <u>little</u> pig.

'Then I'll huff and I'll puff and I'll blow your <u>house</u> in,' said the <u>big</u> bad wolf. So he huffed and he puffed and he blew the <u>house</u> in and ate up the first <u>little</u> pig.

Grouping

Class or group. A group is more satisfactory, particularly when discussing the synonyms as there is more opportunity to contribute.

Materials

A story with a selection of words with readily available synonyms underlined. Take care that synonyms are readily available for the chosen words or you will lose the focus of the procedure.

Procedure

Display some text on the overhead or provide each participant with a copy. Have the class/group read the story together aloud, maintaining a steady and reasonable pace. When they get to an underlined word, have them substitute any word with a similar meaning. Each reader provides his/her own substitution. Note as many of the substitutions as possible. After the reading is completed, return to the substitutions. Write the words given and ask if they make sense and maintain meaning. Discuss why the writer may have chosen the original word and not one of the words substituted. Keeping lists of synonyms on display will provide another resource for children when they are writing. Encourage students to add to the lists when they encounter other synonyms when reading.

The word underlined might be *house*. The children might suggest *home, hut, building*. Is a home exactly the same thing as a house? What about the Houses of Parliament? The word in the text might be *little* and the substitutions *tiny* or *small*. Are they the same? What are the differences in meaning? The more discussion around the words suggested the better. This activity provides some real reasons for referring to a thesaurus or dictionary.

WHO SAID?

Focus: *punctuation*

Rationale

Although this is not strictly speaking a spelling strategy, punctuation is an important part of proofreading so we have included it here. Punctuation conventions are important because they help readers to construct meaning. Text without correct punctuation is difficult to process, especially if it includes direct speech.

Grouping

Whole class, small groups or individuals.

Materials

Copies of a text which includes a conversation and from which the punctuation has been removed. Samples of comic strips.

Procedure

Have children read the text and talk about any difficulties they experience in understanding it. Ask them to underline the direct speech, using a different colour for each speaker. Draw their attention to the way speech is shown in the comic strips. Have them extend the coloured lines to create speech bubbles around the speech in the text. Point out that there is an easier way to do it using inverted commas, which are really stylised speech bubbles. Punctuation related to direct speech is enclosed in the inverted commas, just as it is contained within the speech bubble. Complete the activity by referring children to a variety of texts and allowing them to share the examples they find. There will be variations, so be prepared for discussions about the fact language is generative.

USING POETRY

Every language experience is an opportunity to learn language and learn about language. The most powerful demonstrations, and the most memorable for students of all ages, are those that occur in a meaningful context. Choosing literature carefully and recognising the potential of each example is the key.

Literature provides all the demonstrations about words and language that we would want to make. By helping children to read like writers, we provide them with the opportunity to observe language in action and to notice how language is used in a variety of situations. We are also helping them to develop the skills to observe the irregularities of our language and the changes that are constantly taking place through use. Many of the standards that are now acceptable vary from publisher to publisher, so a student who reads with awareness and a teacher who is alert can make a great many discoveries about language in use.

If teachers are to use literature to demonstrate how language and, in particular, spelling work they must know and love literature as well as language. One of the richest genres to make these demonstrations and to simply enjoy the sounds of the language and use our imagination is poetry. It is not unusual to find teachers with a negative attitude to poetry, uncertain of what to do with it, but it is unusual to find young children with the same attitude. What is important when selecting poetry for classroom use is that the language is well chosen, the imagery vivid, and the rhythm and metre pleasant to the ear. Above all, the sound should reflect the sense of the words. The following examples focus on poetry and offer demonstrations of guiding children to explore language in a number of ways, particularly word meanings and word structures. Use these poems to stimulate and extend children's inherent interest in language. Invite children to play with the words, listen to them, build on them and make them their own. Select appropriate activities from the range provided or develop your own. The emphasis at all times should remain on enjoyment.

Select poetry for the quality and potential of demonstrations, some of which will be planned and some spontaneous. Make sure the activities you plan are fun and not forced and that there are ample times in your classroom when you read just for enjoyment. While it is suggested that you make reference to correct grammatical terms and poetic devices, this should not be laboured. Those children who are ready will absorb the correct terms into their vocabularies; for others this will come later. It is not intended that children be drilled in the terms and/or their meaning, but it is considered important that they be exposed to their correct use in context.

Take time each day just to read poetry as part of your spelling program. Invest in one or two good anthologies and build a classroom collection of the children's favourites. Read what you enjoy. Poetic language, well read and shared enthusiastically, makes for enjoyable listening, regardless of age. Children have a natural sense of fun, delighting in the absurd, the ridiculous and the eccentric. Much of the poetry that is popular with children is therefore nonsense poetry or poetry that plays with words.

The key to each poetry sharing must be enjoyment. The intention is to stimulate children's interest in language, particularly as used in poetic form, not kill it. Poems should not be so dissected that pleasure in them is lost; rather, they should act as springboards to associated language study and play in a memorable context.

Me – Moving

Gordon Winch

I dart and dash,
I jig and jump,
I scamper
 skate and scramble.
I strut and stride,
I slip and slide,
And frequently, I amble.

I leap and lurch,
I crawl and creep,
I rove and romp
 and ramble.
I turn and trip,
I skid and skip,
And now and then –
I gambol.

Talking about language

Introduce the poem to the class or selected group by reading aloud. Invite the group to put it into action. Mime various actions such as *strut, stride, amble.* This may be an opportunity to refer to a dictionary. Ask what kind of words are these? (doing words) What are they describing? (actions) Have children group the verbs with common elements, such as rhyme or similar beginning, for example:

scramb<u>le</u>	stride	slip	creep
amb<u>le</u>	slide	trip	leap
ramb<u>le</u>		skip	
gamb<u>ol</u>			

Asking the students what would happen if they were describing these movements as though they did them yesterday will open up a whole new set of language lessons. *Scramble, amble, ramble* end in '-le'. Why do you think *gambol* ends in '-ol'? *Gamble/gambol*. Meaning?

Same sound, different spelling

Focus attention on those words with similar sounds but different spelling, for example: *creep/leap*. Start a class chart that is on display and accessible so that it can be added to as the children continue to explore the poem and read more widely.

Alliteration

When discussing the poem, direct children's attention to the use of poetic devices to enhance the sound. Children will be quick to notice that in the first five lines of each verse the action words begin with the same sound and even the same sound combinations. For example:

dart and dash
strut and stride

Twistable Turnable Man

Shel Silverstein

He's the Twistable Turnable Squeezable Pullable
Stretchable Foldable Man.
He can crawl in your pocket or fit in your locket
Or screw himself into a twenty-volt socket,
Or stretch himself up to the steeple or taller,
Or squeeze himself into a thimble or smaller,
Yes he can, course he can,
He's the Twistable Turnable Squeezable Pullable
Stretchable Shrinkable Man.
And he lives a passable life
With his Squeezable Lovable Kissable Huggable
Pullable Tugable Wife.
And they have two twistable kids

Who bend up the way that they did.
And they turn and they stretch
Just as much as they can
For this Bendable Foldable
Do-what-you're-toldable
Easily moldable
Buy-what-you're-soldable
Washable Mendable
Highly dependable
Buyable Saleable
Always available
Bounceable Shakable
Almost unbreakable
Twistable Turnable Man.

Introduce the author

This marvellous poem is a wonderful introduction to the world of Shel Silverstein. If there is a particular author you love, this may be a better place to begin. The poem could be used to introduce a thematic unit around the carnival or introduced just for fun. Silverstein's poems provide such wonderful opportunities for exploring language that a collection of his work would be an asset to any spelling program. Ask children to read along with your reading and experiment with different styles as they familiarise themselves with the rhythm and movement of the language. It is an excellent poem to use as a springboard for the exploration of and experimentation with words and word forms. Select from the suggestions of activities or design your own. The keynote should be relevance and enjoyment.

Poet's craft

Talk to children about what they think the main purpose for the poem might be and whether they think it was achieved. Talk about the outstanding features of the poem such as the sound, imagery and humor. Talk about the devices the author has used, and consider which ones were used to good effect in the opinion of the class members. Consider repetition of form, plays on language, alliteration, assonance and internal rhyme.

Playing with words

Discuss and record all the unusual features of the Twistable Turnable Man and his family such as twist, turn, crawl, screw up, shrink and bend. Use any of the words for word study, game playing or word building, if there is an interest or need for a particular group of students.

Suffixes

Have children refer to dictionaries to begin a discussion of the meaning of 'suffix'. List all the words from the poem ending with *able*, and isolate and identify their base words, for example: *twist, turn, stretch*. Discuss what the addition of the suffix *able* does to each base word.

twistable   able to be twisted

turnable   able to be turned

Have children check each listed word for meaning and consistency of spelling, and circle and discuss any that don't seem to fit. Look in anthologies for other poems that focus on *able* and *ible* words. 'Fate's Tools' by Geoffrey Lungren is one.

Now brainstorm words ending in *ible*, for example: *possible, sensible, terrible, horrible*. Ask children to identify the base words. Compare the results with the *able* words. Encourage children to write a generalisation – a sort of class rule – to support them with their spelling. Display this on a chart and note any exceptions already identified. Others can be added as they are discovered through future reading.

Form and tense

In the following two activities, children will need to consider meaning, rhyme, rhythm and metre as well as grammatical construction. Keep the activities lively and lighthearted.

- **Participles**: substitute *ing* for *able*, for example:
  He's the Twisting Turning Squeezing Pulling
  Stretching Folding Man ...

Discuss any changes in spelling and meaning that result.

- **Tense**: substitute *ed* for *able*. Change all the -*able* adjectives to past participles. Read the poem aloud and make other changes necessary to keep the rhyme and rhythm. Discuss the effect of the changes, and talk about whether this new version was successful.

Capitalisation and punctuation

Draw children's attention to the use of capitalisation and punctuation, particularly the lack of commas. Discuss the choices the author has made, and then refer to how these conventions are used in other literature.

4

Strategies for proofreading

In classrooms, proofreading and editing are often referred to almost synonymously, and they are commonly viewed as things that children can do naturally. At best, a proofreading and editing guide will be displayed on the wall. However, both processes can be, and need to be, taught. If we are going to give children the responsibility for the process they undertake when writing, we need to teach them the skills.

In their article 'What brain research says about paying attention', Robert Sywester and Joo-Yun Cho (1993) describe the differences between 'reading' and 'proofreading' in terms of attention processes:

> The focus and intensity of active attention can vary widely. Contrast a proofreader and a cursory reader of a magazine article. The first carefully examines the individual words and punctuation; the second focuses on the general content. When we consciously see such specific information, our attentional system primes itself in anticipation. It increases the response levels of the networks that process that information, and it inhibits other networks. Thus, the proofreader scans a page and spots spelling errors, and the cursory reader skims the same page and spots key content words and phrases.

In the world of commercial publishing, editing and proofreading are carried out at quite different stages of production, although there is some overlap between the two processes. What is referred to in the classroom as 'proofreading' is in fact part of the copyediting process. However, the distinction in terminology is useful in helping teachers and learners to develop the ability to refine meaning and attend to the surface features of text.

In the classroom, **editing** refers to the refining of meaning. The process of editing is usually the first step in preparing a manuscript – a piece of writing – for publication. It includes looking at structure, attending to clarity of meaning, correcting linguistic usage, and styling according to the agreement within the class or school as to what is required for publication.

Proofreading involves approaching writing from a reading stance and making sure that the surface features are standard. It involves all surface features of the text, and includes aspects of editing. The proofreader makes the last check on a piece of work.

Proofreading is a particular kind of reading, requiring concentration on words in their immediate context, rather than on overall meaning. Children must be able to read and be able to recognise non-standard spelling in order to proofread.

It is important that children see proofreading as part of the writing cycle and that they allocate sufficient time for it . What sometimes appears to be poor spelling can in fact be the result of poor writing practices which do not allow appropriate time for proofreading. When writing is done under pressure and proofread immediately, it is highly likely that spelling deviations will not be noticed. The text is familiar and highly predictable, so the reader needs to take up less visual information from the page in order to construct meaning. Asking children to 'correct' their spelling as soon as they have finished writing does not acknowledge what we know about reading and spelling, and often guarantees that they will have non-standard spellings in their texts, not because they cannot spell but because they simply did not see the deviation.

One proofreading technique that writers often find useful is to use a ruler to reveal one line of text at a time so that the reader focuses only on the words on the line. This prevents some of the random eye movements which characterise prediction in reading. It helps the reader to focus on the words on the page rather than read for meaning. Another technique is to point to each word with a pen or pencil, ensuring that the reader reads right to the end of the line.

Teaching procedures

Proofreading and editing should be taught explicitly through the following procedures. Chart the points you have demonstrated and put them on display, making sure that these guides are constructed to meet the needs of the children in your class. Alternatively, each child could have their own editing and proofreading guide that they refer to before presenting final work. The following are offered as suggestions for you to modify and adapt according to the needs of your students.

EDITING GUIDE

The points included on the editing guide/s used in your classroom will depend on the needs of your students. It would be best to individualise the guide provided in figure 10 to meet particular needs.

PROOFREADING GUIDE

The points included on the proofreading guide/s used in your classroom will also depend on the needs of your students. It would be best to individualise the guide provided in figure 11 to meet particular needs. Children need to understand that proofreading is different from reading. When we read we read for meaning. When we proofread we are trying to make it easier for the reader to read our writing. The emphasis is more on the surface features of the text, particularly spelling.

MODELLING

Teacher modelling and modelling other writers are both powerful teaching strategies for demonstrating the processes of editing and proofreading. Talking through what you are doing as you are modelling is important. Collect samples of writing that offer opportunities to highlight particular spelling, punctuation and grammar and use them for modelling purposes.

AUTHOR'S CIRCLE

This procedure that can be useful at several points in the writing process. When children go to the circle with a draft piece of writing and have the opportunity to listen and answer questions posed by the other writers, they actually engage in the editing process. As the writer responds to the meaning-based questions they can add to or delete from their writing orally. When able, children should be encouraged to make notes to ensure the changes are followed through when they return to their writing. If note-taking is not appropriate, ensure that children leave the author's circle to immediately consider and act on the discussion about their piece of writing.

THINK ME A POEM

Writing involves making choices about the surface features of language such as grammatical structures, punctuation and spelling, in order to convey meaning. Free-form poetry frees writers from many surface feature constraints and allows them to choose on the basis of meaning rather than form. This strategy can be used with individuals, small groups or a whole class.

Have children select and then brainstorm a topic. Write each association, phrase, sentence on a separate piece of paper. Have children group ideas in

Figure 10: Example of an editing guide

Editing guide

Ask yourself the following questions when you are ready to publish your writing. You might then like to share your writing with your learning partner or in an authors' circle. The feedback you receive could be very helpful to tighten your writing.

1. Does my piece make sense?
    -   Are there any gaps in the information?
    -   Is there anything more my reader needs to know in order to understand this piece?
    -   Do the events or facts follow each other in proper order or are some parts jumbled?
    -   Are there any parts I need to add or to cut?
    -   Are there any parts I need to change?

2. Are there any words that may be spelt incorrectly? Circle them and check in a dictionary, use word lists in the room or refer to a book where you recall seeing the word.

3. Is each sentence a complete thought?

4. Does each sentence begin with a capital letter and end with a full stop?

5. Are there sentences that ask a question? Do they end with a question mark?

6. Do you have names of people or places in your writing? If so, have you used a capital letter?

7. Do you have characters talking in your writing? Check your use of speech marks.

8. Is the grammar correct? Are nouns, pronouns and verbs in agreement?

9. Is the paragraphing correct? Does each paragraph develop one idea?

Figure 11: Example of a proofreading guide

Proofreading Guide

If you have edited your writing and made the changes necessary, now it is time to prepare your work for publication.

Consider:
- spelling
- punctuation
- handwriting – is your writing clear and are your letters well formed?

If you have used a computer, now is the time to check carefully for typing errors.

1. Place your ruler under each line of text and read line by line, paying attention to each word.

2. Circle the words that you think may be spelt incorrectly.

   - Have you used the have-a-go strategy?

   - Have you used a dictionary?

   - Have you checked word lists around the room?

   - Has a friend checked your spelling?

3. Go back and read again without the ruler to check that the whole piece sounds right.

5. Keep punctuation in mind. Check that you have used capital letters and that commas, full stops, question marks and speech marks are in the correct place. Incorrect punctuation can be distracting for the reader.

Examples of proofreading marks:

⋀	add a letter, word or other material
<u>after</u>	change to a capital letter
⊙	add a full stop
When	start a new paragraph
girl	transpose letters (swap letter positions)
(their)	check spelling
play ground	close up the space

meaningful ways, then present them in a way that conveys that meaning. If this is done as a group or class activity, the brainstorming can be shared. Children will want to start with different ideas and this gives you an opportunity to show that essentially the same surface language can be grouped in different ways to convey different meanings. Once you have demonstrated the procedure, children can do the activity independently, either singly or in groups.

For example, the following collection of phrases:

    mossy paths
    puddles of mud
    misty drizzle
    condensation on the windows
    damp washing
    grey dull day
    everything grey
    smoke from the fire settles on the town
    mist rising from the ground
    cold hands and toes
    red ears and nose

might become:

Winter

Everything grey
Grey dull days.

Condensation on the windows
Mist rising from the ground
Mossy paths and puddles of mud.

Misty drizzle
Damp washing
Everything grey.

Cold hands and toes
Red ears and nose.
Smoke from the fire settles over the town.
Everything grey.

Proofreading activities

In the early stages it is often easier to edit and proofread writing that is unfamiliar. Design proofreading activities to help children focus on particular aspects that you have identified as requiring attention. It may be useful to display some editing symbols which can be introduced to children's personal editing and proofreading guides as they learn them. These symbols are a shorthand way of marking changes or making queries in a text.

Remember that proofreading activities are no substitute for real and purposeful reading and writing activities. If learners are writing for real audiences and purposes they will have real reasons for engaging in editing and proofreading.

The corrected passage for proofreading activity 1:

Drugs

Drugs are things that people take to look cool and tough. Drugs can harm you badly. Drugs aren't just specifically needles, but include coffee, cigarettes, alcohol, medicine and tea. They could all harm your body. By having a lot it goes to your brain and sometimes makes you hyperactive and sometimes wrecks your kidneys. [Discuss use of *wrecks* versus *damages*.]

Aspirin:

Aspirin is a pain relief drug. It helps headaches go away. Doctors have discovered that children under 15 should not take aspirin because their bodies aren't developed enough.

Nicotine:

Nicotine comes in cigarettes and can have side effects. Nicotine makes messages to the brain quicker. You can become addicted to cigarettes and there is also a link between cigarettes and cancer.

PROOFREADING ACTIVITY 1

Imagine that you are an editor and must check the following passage before it goes to press. Mark in the paragraph breaks so that the text is easier to read

DRUGS

Drugs are things that people take to look cool and tough. Drugs can harm you badly. Drugs arn't just specificly needles, but include coffee, cigeretts, alcohol, medecene and tea. They could all harm your body. By having a lot it goes to your brain and sometimes makes you hyper-active and sometimes recks your kidney.

Aspirin:

Aspirin is a pain relief drug. It helps headaches go away. Doctors have discovered that children under 15 should not take aspirin because there bodies aren't devolped enough.

Nicotine:

Nicotine comes in ciggaretts and can have side affects. Nicotine makes messages to the brain quicker. You can become adicted to ciggaretts and their is also a link between ciggaretts and cancer.

PROOFREADING ACTIVITY 2

Imagine that you are an editor and must check the following passage before it goes to press. Circle the non-standard spelling and see if you can find the standard spellings around the room or in a dictionary. Check punctuation and grammar as well.

Why the crab walks sideways

One day long ago in the dreamtime there was a varst dessert and in this dessert there was but one waterhole. This were Jandaberas waterhole. Jandabera is a big crab with large ninners. Over the years more and more aminals came until their were many different aminals living in the dessert. Jandabera was selfish and strong and would not let the other animals drink from the waterhole. Jandabera could run very fast, so finally he agred that if whackara a new little kangaroo could beet him he would share the water hole.

The corrected passage:

Why the crab walks sideways

One day long ago in the dreamtime there was a vast desert and in this desert there was but one water hole. This was Jandabera's water hole. Jandabera is a big crab with large nippers. Over the years more and more animals came until there were many different animals living in the desert. Jandabera was selfish and strong and would not let the other animals drink from the water hole. Jandabera could run very fast, so finally he agreed that if Whackara, a new little kangaroo, could beat him, he would share the water hole.

PROCEDURE FOR DEVELOPING PROOFREADING SKILLS

This proofreading activity is an excellent assessment and learning procedure. Used in place of a traditional dictation which gives limited information on the learner, this procedure can provide insight into the student's control of spelling and punctuation. However, the following chapter deals more fully with assessment and evaluation.

Before the task:

Prepare a copy of the proofreading activity for each student.
Prepare an overhead of the passage.
Ensure that all the children have a red and a blue pencil.

Procedure

Part 1

1. Give each child a copy of the passage.

2. Ask them to write their name, age and class on the page.

3. Make sure all children have a red pencil.

4. Ask children to proofread (or 'correct') the passage. Tell them this means they are to find all the spelling and punctuation that they think is wrong and mark in the correct version. Make sure that you explain the task using language familiar to your students.

Part 2

1. Display the overhead of the passage.

2. Read it out loud.

3. Go through the passage and mark the errors, then show the corrected version.

4. Remove the 'corrected' version from the overhead and ask children to use their blue pencils to mark anything they missed the first time.

5. Collect the proofreading passages.

Analysis

When the passages are collected the following information can be recorded by both teacher and student.

1. The number of 'corrections' made in the first reading (red pen) including spelling and punctuation.

2. The number of 'corrections' made after the demonstration (blue pen) including spelling and punctuation.

3. The number of errors not indicated by the student including spelling and punctuation. That is, any spelling and punctuation overlooked.

5

Assessment, evaluation and reporting

The way we assess and evaluate spelling must operate out of our belief system of how language, and particularly spelling, is learnt. That is, we have to 'measure' what we are teaching. Often in the case of spelling this does not happen. Spelling might be tested as a list of words, ignoring the writing process and the control the student has over the process.

Assessment is the gathering of data on the learning, and evaluation involves the judgments made on that data. The information we gather should be interpreted in ways that inform our practice. In terms of what we want to achieve in teaching spelling, a common outcome might be something like, 'every student is a confident writer and uses standard spelling'. The question is then by what point is this required and expected for each learner. Learning to spell is an ongoing process, but there are certain expectations of schools, parents and communities that need to be taken into account.

The first step in assessing spelling is to place it within the total framework of writing assessment. Figure 12 represents some of the things that may be taken into account when judging writing. Spelling is just one of many, yet our observations in many classrooms suggest that it is the first and major focus once the learner has written something.

In mature writing, the product disguises the process by which it was achieved and there is little point in making such distinction. When evaluating learners, however, we need to be more concerned about their engagement in the process. For example, is what appears to be non-standard spelling the result of genuine difficulties with spelling or a failure of the writer to adequately proofread their work?

Figure 12: Evaluating writing

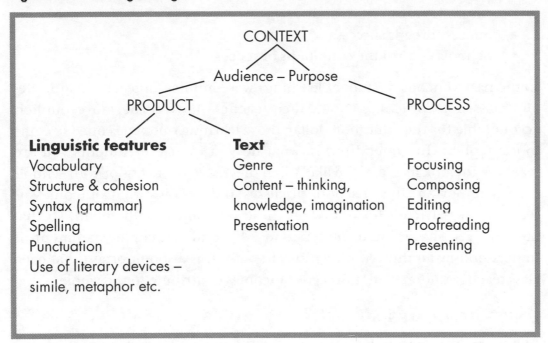

While we have a fairly good understanding of spelling development in the early years of school, we know little about its development beyond years 1 and 2. What should we expect of 9- and 10-year-olds with respect to their spelling? As teachers we need to not only have an understanding of spelling but be aware of our own attitudes towards it.

Outcomes-based education

There is little doubt that standard spelling has assumed an importance beyond the function it plays in written language. It has become the 'ticket' to the literacy club – the heir to the traditions and scholarly world of print. As Yule (1995, p.135) points out:

> The nature of the writing system is related to the values, power relations, and tensions within a society. It has major social and economic consequences … Literacy also involves internalising the social values of a literate community. Spelling is one way to restrict to an elite the initiation into the heritage and the living world of print.

It is not only social attitudes that can affect our teaching and evaluation. Political factors are also at work, and the move to outcomes-based education cannot be ignored. As teachers, we need to consider what this means in relation to teaching language and, in particular, spelling.

Outcomes -based education is based on three basic premises:
- All students can learn and succeed.
- Success breeds success.
- Schools control the conditions of success.

In the past, outcomes (student learning) were implicit in teachers' attitudes and classroom practices. Now, since teachers have to be more publicly accountable for the education dollar, those learning outcomes must become more explicit. In general terms, what do you want the students you are teaching to 'look like' and 'be like' when they leave your class or your school?

It is important that a school discusses and decides what outcomes its teachers are striving for and what these outcomes really mean, so that meaning is shared and understood. A good outcome statement is understood by all those working to achieve it. It is also important that each class teacher understands how class outcomes contribute to the whole.

UNIT OUTCOMES

At a year level, determine outcomes for the unit of work you are planning that will contribute to the achievement of the course outcomes.

ASSESSMENT AND EVALUATION OF OUTCOMES

As a school or a class, determine how you will assess and evaluate the degree to which the outcomes are being achieved. This will be determined by your beliefs about learning. For example, if a spelling test is a chosen mode of evaluation, what information will you be gaining about the learner and what they know about spelling skills? How will this information inform future planning? If spelling is assessed through observing children when writing, by determining the strategies they are using and analysing pieces of writing for example, far more information will be gained about their grasp of spelling, their writing, and their dependence or otherwise on particular spelling strategies.

TEACHING AND LEARNING EXPERIENCES

Identify the teaching and learning experiences you will utilise to move towards the achievement of the outcomes. What would you expect to see your students doing in these learning experiences? A brainstorm of the things you would expect to see will give you indicators of achievement. These are the things that would indicate to you that the students are having success.

Gathering data

There are many ways of gathering information about learners and learning, but within a balanced literacy program the most appropriate assessment will be that based on observation of language users, and the documentation of the growth indicated in children's actual work. How you go about the process will be determined by the purpose of the assessment.

Essentially, assessment is used for three main purposes:

- to analyse the strengths and weaknesses of learners as a basis for planning teaching and learning experiences
- to determine the effectiveness of teaching strategies and resources
- to report on the progress of the learner to all stakeholders – the child, the parent and the system

In the past, writing assessment was very product orientated but, as teachers have become more aware of the process, the pendulum has swung the other way. The product is part of the process and so both aspects of writing are important and both should be assessed. Learners need to be in control of the process in order to achieve the product.

Although distinctions between the writing process and the written product are considered by some researchers as not particularly useful, they have helped teachers rethink traditional attitudes and practices which have focused largely on the product, rather than the process. For this reason it is worth considering writing assessment from these two points of focus.

Assessment is of little value unless the information gathered contributes to the development of more effective learning. Once the data is collected, the next task is to organise and interpret it for effective reporting and for effective programming. Depending on the purpose, information can be gathered in a variety of ways.

PORTFOLIOS

Portfolios can be prepared and organised for a variety of purposes. They are suggested here as one way of organising the information you collect, first for interpretation and discussion with the learner and later with other stakeholders. The information stored in a portfolio should be dated and selected for a particular reason: to show growth or to demonstrate the use of particular strategies in spelling, for example. (In this case they would be called documentary portfolios.)

ANECDOTAL RECORDS

Anecdotal records provide on-the-spot information on a daily basis. They are informal records collected while observing learners as they are writing, or during writing conferences. You might note things such as particular achievements or difficulties, as well as changes in behaviour, attitude and progress since the last observation. Decisions need to be made on how to collect and organise anecdotal information so that it can be interpreted at a more convenient time. From time to time, invite a colleague to offer critical questions which may challenge you to verify your observations and interpretations.

WRITING SAMPLES

Work samples collected over time are essential for determining growth in writing and therefore spelling. A initial dated piece of writing will act as a yardstick to indicate learner development. Loads of work samples become unwieldy and confusing, so they need to be collected at appropriate intervals such as once a month. Particular pieces of work that are noticed can also be added. Before filing, each sample should be quickly analysed by noting particular points observed during the writing process. Particularly in the early stages, the anecdotal records will be very supportive of work samples in recording the sort of behaviour observed during writing and spelling. This would include observing what the child does when they cannot spell a word.

CONFERENCE RECORDS

Much of your ongoing assessment will be through observation. During a writing conference you can focus your observation and keep records of the particular points of discussion based around the student's writing and spelling. These conferences can take place one-to-one or in a small group where you have identified a group of students with similar needs in writing or spelling.

CHECKLISTS

Checklists can be made for the teacher and child and can be useful in monitoring progress. Their form will depend on the purpose of the assessment. They could include comments on general aspects of the writer's behaviour such as 'enjoys writing', 'participates readily', 'can gather information', 'edits and proofreads effectively', 'can write particular kinds of text', and so on. They can also be more specific and relate more closely to aspects of the process such as spelling and spelling strategies, grammar and punctuation. By helping children to keep their own checklists, you can encourage self-assessment and involve the learner in the process. It would be particularly useful to involve students in the development of the checklists .

To the extent that there are certain common outcomes for all children in the class, checklists can be a shorthand way of gathering information on the

Figure 13: Checklist 1

Writing checklist – the process

Focusing

Can the learner focus on selected topics?

Is the range of topics limited?

What interests do they reflect?

Can the learner collect and organise information?

Can the focus be sustained?

Composing

Is the learner willing to write?

Does the learner have spelling strategies to create text?

Does the learner have knowledge of text structure to create text?

Is the range of texts limited?

Editing

Is the learner willing to edit?

Can the learner adopt the stance of a reader to identify points where meaning is lost or information is incomplete?

Can the learner refine meaning and make choices between different ways of saying the same thing?

Proofreading

Can the learner identify non-standard spelling and grammar?

Can the learner standardise non-standard forms?

Are punctuation, sentence, paragraph conventions used appropriately?

indicators of achievement related to those outcomes. Well-designed checklists can be a useful addition to a portfolio in providing specific information.

A checklist must respond to the teaching and learning taking place in the classroom so it is unlikely that a published checklist would be suitable without modifications. Three checklists are included here, two for writing and one for spelling, based on the writing cycle outlined in figure 1 on page 10. You would need to make alterations to suit your particular students.

When the questions on the first writing checklist (figure 13) are examined, it becomes clear that process and product are highly interrelated. It is also obvious that it is of little value addressing problems of editing and proofreading until the learner has some measure of control over focusing and composing.

Since all language is context specific, judgments about writing need to be made in the light of what we know about those contexts. Some judgments, therefore, need to be made about topic, audience, purpose and text type.

The questions in the second checklist (figure 14) will help you to determine in what way the learner has succeeded but will not give you the full picture. There are questions about quality which, in the end, are a matter of teacher judgment. There will be indications of what help is necessary but not why and when such help would be of maximum benefit. To determine why and when appropriate assistance might be given to the learner, some assessment of how the learner engages in the writing process is needed.

Within the context of writing assessment, judgments can also be made about spelling. As spelling is part of writing, attempts to assess it apart from writing are of little value. Assessing spelling through lists of words tells you little more than that the child can spell a particular set of words at a particular time. It does not say anything about the child's ability to use standard spelling and recognise non-standard forms when writing.

Assessing spelling products involves asking questions about the kinds of spelling errors that are being made. Assessing the spelling process means assessing how the writer is using spelling within the writing process.

QUESTIONNAIRES

Questionnaires can be used to reveal student and parent attitudes to writing and spelling. They can be a step towards having children begin to reflect on the learning process with a particular focus, such as spelling.

Developing positive attitudes to writing and spelling are important, and part of your assessment should focus on this. The writer interview is designed

Figure 14: Checklist 2

Writing checklist – the product

Topic

Is the topic appropriate to the audience?

Is there sufficient information or are there things the reader still needs to know?

Are the ideas or events properly sequenced?

Is there coherence? (Related to text type)

Are the ideas original?

Are they presented originally? (Retelling and modelling can be encouraged but copying the work of others – plagiarism – should be discouraged.)

Audience

Who is the audience?

Is the subject matter appropriate to the audience?

Is the language appropriate to the audience?

Is the presentation appropriate to the audience?

- spelling

- punctuation

- grammar

- handwriting

- layout

Has the writing been edited and proofread? (Are spelling, punctuation and grammar appropriate?)

Purpose

What is the purpose of the writing?

Was it achieved? (Did it entertain, inform, persuade, make comparisons, record observations, clarify thinking, predict or hypothesise?)

Text type

Is the learner in control of the text form?

Is the control full or partial? (Can the learner structure and sustain a story, report, letter or play, or does the structure break down?)

Where does the structure break down?

- poor beginning, gives the reader no sense of direction

- story or argument not developed

- lacks conclusion

Which text types has the learner made use of?

Figure 15: Checklist 3

Spelling checklist

The process

Can the learner produce a recognisable spelling of a word?

Is the learner using a variety of spelling strategies?

Is there an over-reliance on one strategy?

Do the spelling strategies used interfere with the process of writing? (This relates to the learner's willingness to take risks with spelling. Those children reluctant to take risks write only what they can spell, or insist on having the spelling before they continue with the writing. The latter disrupts the process of writing.)

Can the learner identify non-standard spelling?

Can the learner correct non-standard spelling? (This involves making use of the strategies such as coming up with alternatives, deciding if a word looks right, using a dictionary to check spelling. The latter also involves knowing how a dictionary is organised.)

Does the learner have the skills to use a dictionary?

The product

Does the learner know the alphabet?

Does the learner know letter–sound correspondences?

- consonants

- vowels

Does the learner repeatedly make the same errors?

Figure 16: Writing and spelling interview

Writing and spelling interview

Do you write at home?
> Often
> Sometimes
> Not very often
> Never

What kind of things do you write at home?

What kind of things do you write at school?

Do you like to write?
> Very much
> It's OK
> Not very much
> I dislike writing

When you are writing and get stuck, what do you do? (If possible, allow the child to define what getting stuck means for him/her.) If the child does not do so, ask:
> What kinds of things cause you problems when you write?
> When you are writing and are interrupted, how do you feel?
> When you are writing and you are interrupted, what do you do?
> What do you do when you want to use a word you cannot spell?
> Do you know someone who is a good writer? Who?
> What makes him/her a good writer?
> Do you know someone who is a good speller? Who? What makes him/her a good speller?
> Do you think he/she ever has a problem when he/she is writing?
> If yes: What do you think he/she does about it?
> If no: Imagine he/she had a problem. What would he/she do about it?
> If someone you knew was having a problem with their writing, how would you help him/her?
> If someone you know was having a problem with their spelling, how would you help?
> What do you think I* would do to help that person?

Is there anything you would like to do better as a writer? Why?

Do you think you are a good writer?
> Yes
> I'm OK
> No

Why/Why not?

Additional comments:

*If someone other than the classroom teacher is conducting the interview, this question should read:
What do you think your teacher would do to help that person?

to assess a writer's attitude to and beliefs about writing. The interview included in figure 16 has been based on the Burke Reader Interview.

SPELLING TESTS

Testing a class list or peer testing of a personal list of words gives you certain information about the learner. It will tell you which particular words that child can spell on that particular day, and this can be translated into a numerical mark, but since we seldom write lists of words this is not very helpful. If you teach spelling in an integrated way, you will need other assessment strategies to give you a picture of how the learner is spelling when writing, the quality of writing, and the control over the writing process.

CLOZE ACTIVITIES

Cloze activities can be teacher-made to focus on spelling. They can be designed to have children focus on beginning, middle or end sounds, on words that sound the same and have different spelling, and on words that sound the same and have the same spelling. Designed well and used for a particular purpose, they can be useful in providing information about children's spelling behaviour.

LEARNING JOURNALS

With practice and teacher modelling, children can use their personal learning journal to describe their learning processes in all areas of learning including spelling. The audience for the journal is usually the teacher and child. An agreement should be made whereby the teacher commits to read and respond to the journal, in writing, on a daily or weekly basis. This is an opportunity for you to engage in a written interaction with the child and gain insight into their view of the learning process.

Student self-evaluation

Children can be helped to build up a list of the strategies they have control of to use when they are writing. From time to time they need to be asked to consider how well they are using the strategies they have identified.

Provide support materials that will help each child to become more active in the assessment and evaluation process. Simple procedures such as assisting children to create a personal list of things they can do when they cannot spell a word can be useful. In all the following examples, modifications need to be made to meet individual needs. They are provided as examples only.

Figure 17: Checklist for self-evaluation

Evaluating your own writing

Good writers have to be able to assess how effective their writing is. Following are some questions to help you think about your writing now that it is complete. Before beginning, you would have focused on your topic, audience and purpose. How successful have you been?

Topic

Have you considered your audience in your choice of topic?

Is the topic interesting?

Have you got enough information about your topic?

Have you got too much information?

Audience

Who are you writing for?

Is your topic suitable for the audience?

Is your language suitable for the audience?

Is your presentation suitable for the audience? Look at your spelling, punctuation, grammar, handwriting and layout.

Have you edited your writing?

Have you proofread your writing?

Are there any words whose spelling you are still unsue of?

Purpose

Why have you written this piece of writing?

Is it to entertain, inform, describe, record observations or to persuade?

Have you been successful?

Text type

Do you know enough about the type of writing you are doing? Find some other examples and make some comparisons.

Have you tried writing a journal, report, letter, directions, narrative, play or poetry?

Figure 18: Checklist for self-evaluation

Keys to better writing/spelling

1. Write every day. Think about the meaning of a word as you are spelling it.

2. Read every day. When reading you may begin to notice how words are spelt and to think about what they mean. This is called reading like a writer.

3. Keep your audience in mind as you write.

4. Select your topic. It is much easier to write about something you know. Do you have enough information to write on your topic? If not, go to the library and read about your topic choice and talk to some other writers and find out what they know.

5. Before beginning, decide the type of writing you are doing. Is it a story, a report or another text type?

6. Work to make your writing clear. Does your writing need tightening?

Good writers often need to write more than one draft. They need to edit their first attempts.

7. Take care with your spelling. Always check your spelling and grammar before presenting your writing to an audience. It must be correct. It is sometimes better to leave this last step for a few days after your have completed your writing.

8. Proofread your writing for spelling and punctuation. Use a dictionary to check words you unsure of.

Figure 19: Checklist of spelling strategies

Things I can do if I cannot spell a word

1. I can use my have-a-go book then try to look it up in the dictionary.

2. I can check my personal dictionary.

3. I can see if the word is around the room or think where I have seen it before.

4. I can ask a friend.

5. I can try to sound it out.

6. I can break it into syllables

7. I can spell it like another word I know.

Interpreting data

When considering your assessment in order to evaluate the success of a learning program, it is important to bear two factors in mind. Firstly, a program should be judged on how well it caters for the individual needs of the learners. All teachers know that children progress at their own rate so that not all children will arrive at the same point at the same time. The important thing is that there is evidence of learning. If you are using an outcomes-based approach you will be making judgments about the achievement of the outcome. If some children have not achieved the outcome you will need to determine whether more time is required or whether a change in approach is necessary to achieve the outcome. Remember, you are working from the belief that all children can learn, so lack of success is not the fault of the student. It may be due to an inappropriate approach or simply not enough time.

Secondly, children who have control of their learning and have rich language programs often achieve far more than you may have expected. For example, the topics they choose to write about may be more sophisticated and imaginative than many teachers would have expected in the past. Because the vocabulary may also be more sophisticated, some children can appear to be worse spellers than they really are. Previously, spelling lists set expectations for spellers. Now there are no limitations set in this form; children are encouraged to spell what they need. There is, however, a strong possibility that parents will expect everything to be spelled 'correctly'. Expectations could become impossibly high unless you clearly define some general expectations at the beginning of the year and convey them to parents.

For parents – most of whom have been taught through traditional approaches to spelling – the Dolch or Schonnell (or similar) lists of most commonly used words, or a list of spelling 'demons' can form the basis of expectations at this level. Such lists are generally to be found in schools but a list of words that you think children would want to be able to spell at this level would suffice. By comparing children's spelling performance in their writing against this list it is possible to show that they are achieving.

Figure 20: Checklist for self-evaluation

Teacher self-evaluation
A self-evaluation checklist for teachers

Am I providing time and choice daily for students to read and write?

Am I providing classroom print that is accessible to all my students?

Am I providing resources to support my students to take responsibility for their spelling?

Do my students have fun with language and words?

Am I an effective reading and writing model for my students?

Am I taking the time on a regular basis to model and demonstrate learning strategies for spelling?

Are my expectations high for all my students?

Are my students involved in the assessment process?

Have I established good communication with the parents of my students?

Are my responses to my students' writing and spelling helpful?

Are the children in my classroom feeling successful, regardless of their abilities?

Am I providing opportunities for students to share and collaborate?

Is the work that students are doing meaningful and purposeful?

Is my approach to spelling consistent with my approach to teaching other aspects of language?

Are my evaluation approaches consistent with my philosophy and my teaching?

(Adapted from Regie Routman, 1991, *Blue Pages Resources*)

6

Teaching strategies and classroom organisation

There appear to be four components to be considered in a balanced program to help writers to become standard spellers:

- creating an appropriate environment
- encouraging risk-taking
- sensitising learners to words in context
- developing proofreading skills

Before embarking on any teaching strategies, you must determine the needs of your students through effective assessment and evaluation which is compatible with your approach to teaching language. Developing an understanding of how language is learned and hence how spelling is learned is the beginning. We then need to explore the range of teaching strategies available to us to implement our beliefs.

The introduction of national profiles and outcomes-based education has directed teachers' attention to how we organise ourselves to 'get the job done'. If outcomes-based education is about every child succeeding and learning, and about meeting individual needs, then the implications for the organisation of schools and classrooms are enormous. We have to look beyond traditional organisation and use strategies that will provide flexibility and enhance learning for all the students in a particular class.

A class of students represents a tremendous range of abilities. Whether it is a composite class, multi-age grouping or a graded class, we all know the challenge that presents itself for us in meeting the needs of all. The approaches described below are well documented and need little introduction. They are described here in the light of current changes in education and particularly with the teaching of literacy in mind. The introduction and continuation of any of these strategies is determined by effective assessment and evaluation. Knowing what each student is doing and, in the case of spelling, being aware of strengths and weaknesses and of the learning strategies they are using are central to the choices you make as you go about organising and managing your classroom.

Try out some of the strategies and view what happens critically. If they are already in place, view what you see with a critical eye. Video some lesson segments and look at them quietly at the end of the day, preferably with a supportive colleague. While it is crucial to critically evaluate the effectiveness of any management and organisational strategies you have in place, you also need to think about what is there that will allow these things to work. Asking children to work cooperatively, to respect each other, and to work independently will not necessarily guarantee that these things happen. Skills are required and we need to teach these to our students, and time to set up an environment where such things can take place is an essential part of the process. Some of the considerations are:

- integrating the curriculum
- cooperative learning strategies
- peer tutoring
- learning centres
- learning contracts
- organising resources

INTEGRATING THE CURRICULUM

All reading lessons, object lessons, grammar, history, geography, may be made vehicles for improving the knowledge of your pupils in this subject [spelling]. From five to ten minutes at the close of reading lessons should frequently be devoted to spelling, all misspelled words should be placed on the blackboard, and finally the blackboard notes should be carefully revised.
(NSW Educational Gazette, vol . 1, no. 7, 1891.)

While we have come a long way in our understandings about the teaching of spelling and integration since 1891, we need to keep in mind the daily opportunities that occur for integration. Spelling must be integrated since it is an integral part of reading and writing, and spelling activities should be a natural consequence of reading and writing. Literature and children's own writing provide opportunities for learning about spelling. When spelling is taught in this way, the emphasis is always on meaning and effective communication, not on spelling in isolation from its purpose.

Integration is not just about integrating spelling into the language program but about integrating all learning. Integration is only possible when the teacher's planning is explicit and there are clear purposes for the choices made concerning teaching/learning experiences, grouping of students and resources. Teachers wanting to explore an approach to integration should refer to *The Big Picture* by Pigdon and Woolley 1992.

In essence, integrating the curriculum involves the integration of content and process. The content subjects are essentially concerned with ideas about how the world works. The process subjects offer a range of ways of allowing us to represent how we see and make meaning of our worlds (real or imagined). Michael Halliday's model of the ways in which language is used can help us to understand this notion of content and process subjects. Halliday (1982) says that when we use language, we learn language, we learn through language and we learn about language.

Language and maths are process subjects while the remainder of the curriculum is related largely to content for developing language and maths and vice versa. Much of what passes for integrated learning is often no more than a set of subject related activities bound by a common theme. Although thematic approaches may be integrated, they are not necessarily so.

COOPERATIVE LEARNING

Cooperative learning can take many forms, and there is a great deal written on the subject. Setting up a physical environment in which students can work cooperatively involves thought and planning, from the arrangement of the classroom itself, to the organisation of groups, to the general attitude to learning that the teacher instils in the students. These principles must apply from day one when the children arrive, and be consistent with daily events. Children must have the chance to get used to working together (particularly if they have not had this experience in previous years) and develop tolerance for each other as they build a learning community. There are several good books to help get started and maintain a cooperative learning environment, for example: *The Collaborative Classroom: A Guide to Co-operative Learning* (Hill & Hill 1990).

In the early years, children have to learn how to work in groups, consider each other and do simple things such as taking turns, long before you send them off to work in this way. One way of establishing group work is to encourage discussion in groups of about five. Establishing a routine and developing 'rules' ensures that students all have a clear purpose. They need to know and experience what it looks like, feels like and sounds like to work together in this way. It is important to continue to model cooperative behaviors as a support to learners.

Figure 21: A model of integrated learning

A model of integrated learning

Information	Nature of activity	Subjects involved
Facts	*Prior knowledge* • making predictions • asking questions	
	Shared experience • observation • collection information/data	*Learning about* • social education • science • environmental education • personal development • technology studies
Concepts	*Processing information* • listing • grouping • categorising • classifying • labelling • organising ideas	*Learning through* • language • art • drama • mathematics • movement • music
Generalisations	*Synthesising* • making statements • generalising • looking for relationships	*Learning about* • social education • science • environmental education • personal development • technology studies
Further information	*Refinement and extension of knowledge* • elaborating • justifying • reflecting	

(from K. Pigdon & M. Woolley, *The Big Picture*, p.9)

Once these procedures are in place, they will support students in cooperative approaches to learning to spell. In the process of writing there will be many opportunities to work together, particularly when drafting, jointly constructing text, editing and proofreading. Students will be more able to use procedures such as peer testing of spelling and to engage in activities involving the exploration of words if they are established in a cooperative working environment.

PEER TUTORING

As part of your spelling program, there may be times when you would consider the use of peer tutoring to develop the writing and spelling skills of particular children. Alternatively, it may involve children working together to proofread personal or other texts. If the children are carefully selected and matched appropriately, there can be benefits for both as a consequence of working together.

In order for peer tutoring to be successful, the tutor and tutee must be trained to participate and to understand what is expected of them. For the purposes of developing spelling skills, the tutor would be trained to guide a learner writer through a writing experience and would be aware of some strategies to assist the tutee with their ideas and with their spelling. If the situation is carefully arranged, a positive relationship will soon develop between the two parties, resulting in benefits for both children. Note that peer tutoring should be carefully monitored to ensure progress for the children involved.

LEARNING CENTRES

The physical environment is an important part of supporting learners to learn to work independently, cooperatively and as a whole class. As far as spelling is concerned, organisation of resources is of great importance. As children go about their daily writing, they need to be able to rely on the fact that they can easily find the resources they need. If they have to search for dictionaries, class-generated word lists, books, writing implements and the like, they will soon lose enthusiasm.

As well as aiding the general organisation of resources, learning centres can contribute to individual learning. Often compromises have to be made as the space is too small; however, we need to be as creative as possible to provide spaces to set up designated learning centres where small group and individual activities can take place. Your centres will be flexible and will change due to space constraints, but at various times would include a reading corner, a writing centre, a listening centre and other centres associated with a particular curriculum area, topic or process.

These centres provide an opportunity to help students appreciate that reading and writing and, of course, spelling are part of all learning, regardless of the curriculum area in focus. The centre can be set up with resources that will reinforce the spelling skills required, no matter what the learning experience is. It will be a chance to focus on the audiences and purposes for writing, and it is the development of this understanding that will impact on a child's use of standard spelling.

LEARNING CONTRACTS

Once your environment is set up and the students are familiar with the procedures, you are ready to introduce group work and learning contracts.

Task boards provide an excellent organisational aid for supporting the learner and assisting the teacher to be sure they are providing a balanced program. The type of activities on the task board will depend on your class and should be introduced gradually as you familiarise the group with each activity and expectations.

ORGANISING RESOURCES

For children to learn to read and write and spell, the resources in the classroom are important. Most important are the books. You need books for independent, guided and shared reading. You need good books and lots of books, so that children have choice. It is crucial that your groups or individuals are interacting with a text in guided reading that is appropriate and is of interest to them. If you provide individual book boxes for children for their independent reading, the books should be selected for each child so they have plenty of opportunity to use their reading skills and do not have to struggle with the text. Children should experience success. For shared reading, select various texts types which provide the opportunity to make planned demonstrations to the group or class.

Developing programs and policies

Developing a spelling program demands the same understandings as developing a program in any learning area. While spelling cannot be separated from the other aspects of learning language, we have to be explicit in our planning, so that we can then be explicit in our teaching. We must begin by clearly articulating our understandings about language and learning on which we can build our programs for reading, writing, listening and talking. We argue that you have to focus on each of these things separately within your understanding about their inter-relatedness. If not we risk sloppy teaching. Incidental teaching is not accidental teaching. Our students will not learn by accident and we must plan the main focus of our teaching to meet the outcomes set in our particular situation.

We must know our students well and take this information with us as we engage in our planning. It is impossible to use last year's program, as each year our students are different and bring different strengths and weaknesses. We have to be prepared to tailor a program to genuinely meet children's needs, therefore we argue no published program will be adequate. The final aspect is the assessment and evaluation, although it is difficult to say if this comes before or after planning. We argue that these are almost inseparable and neither one can exist without the other. Therefore the spelling program will continually be adjusted and modified in the light of the assessment and evaluation taking place. What you do in writing and spelling must be consistent with what you do in other aspects of language.

CONCLUSION

Until you have an effective writing program in place, it is not appropriate to look at changing your approach to teaching spelling. Without all the elements in place, children would not be supported in learning spelling and would struggle. Consider how effective your modelling is, how often and well you make demonstrations about spelling across all key learning areas and the usefulness of the information about spelling you are collecting through your assessment procedures. Children need to develop knowledge of sounds and letters, spelling consciousness, a love of language, and an understanding of the purposes of reading, writing and spelling in and out of the classroom. The program should include specific strategies that will meet the needs of students whether or not they are beginning or more experienced writers.

No program or series of activities can guarantee that every child learns to spell. Learning is a complex social and psychological activity, much of which may be determined outside the classroom. It seems to us that there is little use in being able to spell unless you engage in reading and writing. Interestingly, many who would class themselves as poor spellers manage to become highly successful and productive members of society because poor spelling has not prevented them from actively engaging in reading and writing. They have recognised their limitations and work within them. An integrated program prevents, as far as is possible, spelling becoming a barrier to reading and writing.

References and further reading

Bartch, J. 1992, 'An alternative to spelling: An integrated approach', *Language Arts*, vol. 69, October, pp. 404–8.

Bean, W. & Bouffler, C. 1987, *Spell by Writing*, Primary English Teaching Association, Sydney.

Bissex, G, 1980, *Gnys At Wrk: A child Learns to Read and Write*, Harvard University Press, Cambridge MA.

Bouffler, C. 1984, Case study explorations of functional strategies in spelling, unpublished doctoral dissertation, Indiana University, Bloomington.

Callaway, B., McDaniel, H. & Mason, G.E. 1972, 'Five methods of teaching language arts: A comparison', *Elementary English*, vol. 49, pp.1240–5

Cambourne, B. 1995, 'Towards an educationally relevant theory of literacy learning: Twenty years of inquiry', *The Reading Teacher*, vol. 49, no.3, November, pp. 183–90

Beers, J.W. & Henderson, E.H. 1977, 'A study of developing orthographic concepts among first graders', *Research in the Teaching of English*, vol.11, pp. 133–48.

Clay, M. 1991, *Becoming Literate: The Construction of Inner Control*, Heinemann, Auckland.

Beeching, C.L. 1983, *Exploring Words: A Dictionary of Eponyms*, Oxford University Press, Oxford.

Emmitt, M. & Hornsby, D. 1996, 'Phonics in early literacy', in *Practically Primary*, Australian Literacy Educators Association, Melbourne.

Gee, J. 1991, 'What is literacy?' in *Rewriting Literacy*, eds C. Mitchell & K. Weller, Beigin & Garvey, New York.

Gentry, R. & Gillet, J.W. 1993, *Teaching Kids to Spell*, Heinemann, Portsmouth NJ.

Halliday, M.A.K. 1982, 'Three aspects of children s language development: Learning language, learning through language, learning about language', in *Oral and Written Language Research: Impact on the Schools*, eds Y. Goodman, M. Haussler & D. Strickland, National Council of Teachers of English, Urbanna, Ill.

Halliday, M.A.K. 1984, *Language as Social Semiotic: The Social Interpretation of Language and Meaning*, Edward Arnold, London.

Hammill, D.D., Larsen, S. & McNutt, G.1977, 'The effects of spelling instruction: A preliminary study', *Elementary School Journal*, vol. 78, pp.67–72.

Harste, J., Burke, C. & Woodward, V. 1984 *Language Stories and Literacy Lessons*, Heinemann, Portsmouth NJ.

Hill, S. & Hill, T. 1990, *The Collaborative Classroom: A Guide to Co-operative Learning*, Eleanor Curtain, Melbourne.

Mulcaster, R. 1582, cited in *Spelling*, G.H. Vallins, Andre Deutsch, London, 1965.

Pigdon, K. & Woolley, M. (eds) 1992, *The Big Picture: Integrating Children's Learning*, Eleanor Curtain, Melbourne.

Read, C. 1975, *Children's Categorisation of Speech Sounds in English*, National Council of Teachers of English, Urbanna.

Routman, R. 1994, *Invitations: Changing as Teachers and Learners K–12*, Heinemann, Portsmouth NJ.

Sadler, B.R. 1981, *Spelling Matters* Jacaranda Press, Brisbane.

Silverstein, S. 1981, *A Light in the Attic*, Harper & Row, New York.

Smith, E. n.d., *An Accidental History of Words: A Lighthearted Look at the Things We Say*, Bay Books, Sydney.

Smith, F. 1978, *Understanding Reading: A Psycholinguistic Analysis of Reading and Learning to Read*, Holt, Rinehart & Winston, New York.

Stanhope, P.D. 4th Earl of Chesterfield 1932, *Letters to His Son*, vol. 4, Oxford University Press, Oxford.

Sywester, R. & Cho, J. 1992/3, 'What brain research says about paying attention', *Educational Leadership*, Dec/Jan.

Templeton, S. 1992, 'New trends in an historical perspective: Old story, new resolution – sound and meaning in spelling', *Language Arts*, vol. 69, no. 6, October, pp. 454 – 62

Walker, D. & Brown, P. 1994, *Pathways to Co-operation: Starting Points for Co-operative Learning*, Eleanor Curtain, Melbourne.

Wilde, S. 1992, *You Kan Red This: Spelling and Punctuation for Whole Language Classrooms*, K–6, Heinemann, Portsmouth NJ.

Yule, V. 1995, 'The politics of spelling', in *The Multicultural Imperative*, ed. D. Meyers, Phadrus Books, Sydney.

Index

alphabet strips 28
anecdotal records 69–70
approximation 22
assessment 66–7
attitudes to writing and
    spelling 1–8, 72
audience and purpose 26, 31
author's circle 31–2, 57

beliefs about learning 23
bundling 42–44

checklists 70–2, 77–9, 80
classroom environment 85–6
classroom print 27–8
cloze activities 44, 45, 46–7
conditions of learning 19–22
conference records 70
context 25
cooperative learning 83–5

daily writing 29
demonstration 20
dialogue journals 37–8

editing 26, 55–6
editing guide 57, 58
engagement 20–1
evaluation 66–7
expectation 21

games 29
guided reading 33

immersion 20
integrated approach 12, 24,
    25, 82–3, 84
invented spelling 14–15, 26

learning
    centres 85–6
    contracts 86
    environment 27–9

journals 76
letter manipulation 28
linguistic data pool 14
look, cover, write, check 30

misspellings 6
modelling 30, 38–40, 57
myths and misconceptions
    3–8

non-standard spellings 7

observation 69
opportunities for writing 28–9
outcomes-based education
    67–9, 79, 81

peer tutoring 85
personal dictionaries 31
phonetic spelling 4, 15
phonics 6, 25, 29
picture writing 40–1
poetry 32, 50–4, 57
portfolios 69
proofreading 7, 19, 26, 55–65
    activities 61–5
    guide 57, 59
punctuation 49
purposeful opportunities
    21–2

questionnaires 72–6

reading and spelling 7, 9–11,
    18
responding to children's
    writing 22, 31
risk-taking 30
role of learner 21, 27
role of teacher 27

self-assessment 70–2, 73, 74,
    76

self-evaluation 76–9, 80
shared reading 33
spell checks 33
spelling
    development 17, 25
    lists 5, 9, 24–5, 66, 72, 79
    principles 13
    programs 24–6, 86–7
    and reading and writing
      9–11, 18
    reform 1–2
    strategies 17, 79
    tests 68, 76
standard spellers 18, 81
standard spelling 5–6, 16–19
story schema 41
synonym substitution 47–9

teaching strategies
    to develop proofreading
      55–64
    to encourage risk-taking
      35–44
    to encourage writing 35–44
    to sensitise learners to
      words in context 44–54
teaching spelling 11–12
text schema 42

writing and spelling 9–11, 18
    interview 75
writing folders 32
writing process 10–11, 32
writing samples 70

written conversation 35–7